THE LIVING CO

INALIENABLE RIGHTS SERIES

The Living Constitution

David A. Strauss

UNIVERSITY PRESS

2010

OXFORD
UNIVERSITY PRESS

Oxford University Press, Inc., publishes works that further
Oxford University's objective of excellence
in research, scholarship, and education.

Oxford   New York
Auckland   Cape Town   Dar es Salaam   Hong Kong   Karachi
Kuala Lumpur   Madrid   Melbourne   Mexico City   Nairobi
New Delhi   Shanghai   Taipei   Toronto

With offices in
Argentina   Austria   Brazil   Chile   Czech Republic   France   Greece
Guatemala   Hungary   Italy   Japan   Poland   Portugal   Singapore
South Korea   Switzerland   Thailand   Turkey   Ukraine   Vietnam

Copyright © 2010 by Oxford University Press, Inc.

Published by Oxford University Press, Inc.
198 Madison Avenue, New York, New York 10016

www.oup.com

Oxford is a registered trademark of Oxford University Press.

Library of Congress Cataloging-in-Publication Data
Strauss, David A.
The living Constitution / David A. Strauss.
p.   cm.
Includes index.
ISBN 978-0-19-537727-9
1. Constitutional law—United States.
2. Constitutional history—United States.   I. Title.
KF4550.S78   2010
342.7302–dc22   2009038237

Printed in the United States of America
on acid-free paper

For my family

Acknowledgments

MANY COLLEAGUES, FRIENDS, and students have discussed with me, over the years, the issues that I address in this book and have helped me with articles I have written on these subjects. I owe particular thanks to Geoffrey Stone for the invitation to contribute to the Inalienable Rights series, and to him and Cynthia Jurisson for their detailed and very helpful suggestions on the manuscript. Some of the chapters of this book are substantially revised versions of the following articles and book chapters: "Common Law Constitutional Interpretation," 63 *University of Chicago Law Review* 877 (1996); "The Irrelevance of Constitutional Amendments," 114 *Harvard Law Review* 1457 (2001); "Freedom of Speech and the Common-Law Constitution," in Lee C. Bollinger & Geoffrey R. Stone, eds., *Eternally Vigilant: Free Speech in the Modern Era* (University of Chicago Press, 2002); "Common Law, Common Ground, and Jefferson's Principle," 112 *Yale Law Journal* 1717 (2003); and "The Common Law Genius of the Warren Court," 49 *William and Mary Law Review* 845 (2007).

Editor's Note

We hold these truths to be self-evident, that all men are created
equal, that they are endowed by their Creator with certain unalien-
able Rights....

—*THE DECLARATION OF INDEPENDENCE*

In this, the ninth, volume of The Inalienable Rights series, David
Strauss explores the process of constitutional interpretation and the
very meaning of the Constitution itself. In recent decades, lawyers,
scholars, and judges have debated the wisdom and legitimacy of
competing modes of constitutional interpretation. Phrases like
"original intent," "judicial restraint," "strict construction," "judicial
activism," and "living Constitution" have been bandied about in law
reviews, Supreme Court opinions, newspaper editorials, and presidential debates. They embody, or purport to embody, different
visions of what we expect of our judges and of our Constitution.

In *The Living Constitution*, Strauss argues that the very idea of a
static Constitution grounded in a narrow conception of "original"

meaning is both incoherent and indefensible. Any reasoned conception of constitutional law must encompass a recognition that the substantive understanding of the Constitution must change over time with changes in technology, demography, economics, and politics. But if we have a "living" Constitution whose meaning can justifiably change over time, how do we maintain the legitimacy of constitutional law? If we are committed to the rule of law, then judges must not have unbridled authority to interpret the Constitution in any way that suits their fancy. How can we achieve the benefits of adaptability without opening ourselves up to the dangers of judicial manipulation?

It is Strauss's thesis that we have ingeniously solved this dilemma by evolving a form of constitutional "common law," in which judges are constrained not by an artificially rigid commitment to "originalism," but by a method that has been part of Anglo-American law for centuries—the adherence to the values of tradition and precedent. Strauss argues that through this unique process of constitutional common law the Supreme Court can successfully walk the fine line between stability and change.

After identifying what he sees as the deficiencies of "originalism," Strauss explores the general theory of constitutional common law and then illustrates his concept of the living Constitution by examining two fundamental developments in American constitutional law: the evolution of the doctrine of freedom of speech and the evolution of the law governing racial discrimination. He then takes on what he acknowledges to be a particularly difficult issue: *Roe v. Wade*. Strauss concludes that the abortion decision may be indefensible under an "originalist" view of the Constitution, but it is defensible within the framework of the living Constitution.

In *The Living Constitution*, Strauss takes on some of the most difficult and important issues of constitutional law today. In giving content to specific constitutional rights, whether it be that "Congress shall make no law...abridging the freedom of speech," of "no person shall be deprived of life, liberty or property without due process of law," or no State shall deny any person "the equal protection of the laws," we need a principled approach to interpretation. Strauss offers an original, perceptive, and compelling explanation of the approach that has dominated constitutional law for the past century.

Geoffrey R. Stone

Contents

CONTENTS

THE LIVING CONSTITUTION

Introduction

Do We Want a Living Constitution?

DO WE HAVE a living constitution? Do we want to have a living constitution? A "living constitution" is one that evolves, changes over time, and adapts to new circumstances, without being formally amended. On the one hand, the answer has to be yes: there's no realistic alternative to a living constitution. The written U.S. Constitution, the document under glass in the National Archives, was adopted more than 220 years ago. It can be amended, but the amendment process is very difficult. The most important amendments were added to the Constitution almost a century and a half ago, in the wake of the Civil War, and since that time many of the amendments have dealt with relatively minor matters.

Meanwhile, the world has changed in incalculable ways. The United States has grown in territory, and its population has multiplied several times. Technology has changed, the international situation has changed, the economy has changed, social mores have changed—all in ways that no one could have foreseen when the

Constitution was drafted. And it is just not realistic to expect the cumbersome amendment process to keep up with these changes.

So it seems inevitable that the Constitution will change, too. This is a good thing, because an unchanging constitution would fit our society very badly. Either it would be ignored or, worse, it would be a hindrance, a relic that would keep us from making progress and prevent our society from working in the way it should.

On the other hand, there seem to be many reasons to insist that the answer to that question—do we have a living constitution that changes over time?—cannot be yes. In fact, the critics of the idea of a living constitution have pressed their arguments so forcefully that, among people who write about constitutional law, the term "living constitution" is hardly ever used, except derisively. The U.S. Constitution is supposed to be a rock-solid foundation, the embodiment of our most fundamental principles: that's the whole idea of having a constitution. Public opinion may blow this way and that, but our basic principles—our constitutional principles—must remain constant. Otherwise, why have a constitution at all?

There's an even bigger problem with the living Constitution, or so it might seem. A living constitution is, surely, a manipulable constitution. If the Constitution is not constant—if it changes from time to time—then someone is changing it. And that someone is changing it according to his or her own ideas about what the Constitution should look like. The "someone," it's usually thought, is some group of judges. So a living constitution would not be the Constitution at all; in fact it is not even law any more. It is just a collection of gauzy ideas that appeal to the judges who happen to be in power at a particular time and that they impose on the rest of us.

So it seems we want to have a constitution that is both living, adapting, and changing and, simultaneously, invincibly stable and impervious to human manipulation. How can we escape this predicament?

The good news is that we *have* mostly escaped it, albeit unself-consciously. Our constitutional system, without our fully realizing it, has tapped into an ancient source of law, one that antedates the Constitution itself by several centuries. That ancient kind of law is the common law. The common law is a system built not on an authoritative, foundational, quasi-sacred text like the Constitution. Rather, the common law is built out of precedents and traditions that accumulate over time. Those precedents allow room for adaptation and change, but only within certain limits and only in ways that are rooted in the past. Our constitutional system— I'll maintain—has become a common law system, one in which precedent and past practices are, in their own way, as important as the written U.S. Constitution itself. A common law constitution is a "living" constitution, but it is also one that can protect fundamental principles against transient public opinion. And it is not one that judges (or anyone else) can simply manipulate to fit their own ideas.

The bad news is that, perhaps because we do not realize what a good job we have done in solving the problem of how to have a living constitution, inadequate and wrongheaded theories about the Constitution persist. One theory in particular—what is usually called "originalism"—is an especially hardy perennial. Originalism is the antithesis of the idea that we have a living constitution. It is the view that constitutional provisions mean what the people who adopted them—in the 1790s or 1860s or whenever—understood them to mean. (There are different forms of originalism, but this characterization roughly captures all of them.) In the hands of its most aggressive proponents, originalism simply denies that there is any dilemma about the living Constitution. The Constitution requires today what it required when it was adopted, and there is no need for the Constitution to adapt or change, other than by means of formal amendments.

There is something undeniably natural about originalism. If we're trying to figure out what a document means, what better place to start than with what the authors understood it to mean? Also, as a matter of rhetoric, everyone is an originalist sometimes: when we think something is unconstitutional—say, widespread electronic surveillance of American citizens—it is almost a reflex to say something to the effect that the "founding fathers" would not have tolerated it. And there are undoubtedly times when originalism is the right way to approach a constitutional issue. But when it comes to difficult, controversial constitutional issues—such as whether the Constitution forbids discrimination against minorities and women or, to give a recent example, whether a local government has the power to ban handguns—originalism is a totally inadequate approach. It is worse than inadequate: it hides the ball by concealing the real basis of the decision.

In the first chapter of this book, I will discuss originalism and show why its view of the Constitution—as an unchanging document whose meaning was determined when it was ratified—should be rejected. But you can't beat somebody with nobody, and if the idea of a living constitution is to be defended, it is not enough to show that the competing theory is badly flawed. So, in the rest of the book, I will describe and defend the approach that I think is at the core of our constitutional tradition—our living constitutional tradition—an approach derived from the common law and based on precedent and tradition. That approach addresses the issues that have been raised by the critics of the living constitution. It shows how the Constitution can evolve and yet still provide the solid principles that a constitution should provide—and not become the plaything of judges.

In chapter 2, I will describe the common law approach: how it works and why it might be justified. Then, in chapters 3 and 4, I will show how two of the most important developments in our constitutional system are the products not of the text of the Constitution, and not of the original understandings, but of a common law approach to the Constitution. That is, they are products of a living constitution. Chapter 3 is about freedom of speech—the First Amendment, as we usually say, although the point is that much more is involved than those lines of constitutional text. Chapter 4 describes how racial segregation became unconstitutional, in the case of *Brown v. Board of Education*—the most famous case of the last hundred years, or more, and for many people the Supreme Court's, and maybe the Constitution's, finest hour. But the story of *Brown* is not a story about the words of the Constitution, nor about the views of the people who drafted and ratified its provisions. It is a story about the evolutionary common law processes of the living Constitution.

In chapter 5, I will turn back to the written Constitution, the one in the National Archives. The living Constitution is a central part of our law, but it is only a part. The written Constitution remains absolutely crucial. The problem is how to reconcile the two: how we can have both a static written constitution and a dynamic living constitution in the same system. I will explain the vital role that the written Constitution plays in our system, and how that role complements our evolving, living Constitution. Then, since the idea behind a living constitution is that the Constitution must change, in chapter 6 I will explain how the living Constitution fits together with the formal amendment process that the written Constitution prescribes. The amendment process is, perhaps surprisingly, nearly irrelevant. It is the living Constitution that is responsible for keeping the U.S. Constitution from becoming obsolete, or worse.

CHAPTER ONE

Originalism and Its Sins

WHY CAN'T WE JUST READ THE WORDS?

At first, it seems that interpreting the Constitution cannot be such a difficult thing to do. The document is short—even shorter than it appears, if we leave out provisions that are never invoked today—and mostly written in plain English. Why not just do what the words say?

Sometimes we can. Many provisions of the U.S. Constitution are quite precise and leave no room for quarreling, or for fancy questions about interpretation. The president must be thirty-five years old. Each state shall have two senators. Members of Congress take office on January 3 of the year after an election; the president takes office on January 20. Senators are elected every six years, representatives every two, the president every four.

Those provisions, by and large, do not generate a lot of controversy. We really can do just what the words say. Law professors could come up with hypothetical situations that might uncover hidden ambiguities or uncertainty in the words, because law professors are paid to do things like that. But those situations are likely to remain hypothetical, and the words tell us, pretty much exactly, what to do in the real world.

But other provisions of the Constitution, while written in plain enough English, do not give us such unequivocal instructions. The First Amendment says that "Congress shall make no law...abridging the freedom of speech." Those words don't seem especially obscure or technical, and some important figures in the history of American law have claimed that, as with the provision about the president's being thirty-five, all we have to do is follow the plain meaning of the First Amendment. That was the position, notably, of Justice Hugo Black, one of the intellectual leaders of the Supreme Court during the 1950s and 1960s, when the Court greatly expanded the civil rights and civil liberties of Americans. When Justice Black was asked a question about what the First Amendment required, he was fond of pulling a copy of the Constitution out of his pocket (a well-worn copy, of course) and reading it aloud. I think "no law" means *no law*, he would say: what do you think it means?

Justice Black's way of dealing with the First Amendment was certainly rhetorically effective; it has adherents today; and Justice Black was in many ways a force for good. But the fact is that, when we're dealing with the First Amendment—and other provisions of the Constitution about which people actually argue, and bring lawsuits—just reading the words is not remotely enough. OK, "no law" means no law; let's stipulate that. But what is "the freedom of speech"? Surely it does not include the freedom to make harassing phone calls, or to scream into the ear of a cardiac patient, or to transmit military secrets to an enemy agent. Does it include the freedom to post pornography on the internet in, let's say, a way that is especially attractive to children? Or to spread false rumors about a person running for public office? Or to publish truthful information that grievously invades the privacy of an ordinary citizen? You can squint at the words as hard as you want, and you won't get an answer to those questions.

And what does "abridging" mean? Does it include laws that deny public funds to a speaker? So if the National Endowment for the Humanities denies me a grant to stage a play I have written, because it's a bad play, has the NEH violated my First Amendment rights? Obviously not. But what if it denies someone a grant because her play criticizes the president? That looks a lot more problematic. But looking up the word "abridge" in the dictionary won't tell you that, or tell you how to draw the line between acceptable and unacceptable denials of public subsidies. And then there is the first word of the First Amendment, which is "Congress"; so the courts, or the president, or the city of Chicago can freely abridge my freedom of speech? That can't be right, and, under clearly established law, it is not right. But that established law isn't derived from the words alone.

Many other provisions of the Constitution raise similar questions. If a state forbids gay men and lesbians from being nursery school teachers, does that state deny "equal protection of the laws," in violation of the Fourteenth Amendment? If police officers search a car that has been stopped just for a minor traffic violation, is that an "unreasonable search," which the Fourth Amendment forbids? The list of questions like this—ones that cannot be settled just by reading the words of the Constitution—is long, and these questions are the ones that are disputed in the courts and in society at large.

Having said all of that about the provisions of the Constitution whose implications are not clear, we have to be careful to recognize how important the clear provisions of the Constitution are. It is a very good thing that we know precisely when one president leaves office and another takes over; imagine the mess it would create if the Constitution said that the presidential succession occurs "at an appropriate time," or that presidents should serve terms not of four years, as they do now, but of "a number of years commensurate with the national interest." The point is not that everything in the Constitution is subject to varying interpretations, or that the clear provisions are trivial; they most certainly are not. But the provisions of the Constitution that get fought over, inside and outside the courts, are not so clear.

ORIGINALISM

When we are dealing with one of the provisions that is not so clear, how should we go about deciding what the Constitution requires? One view—the view that is commonly called "originalism"—gives an answer that seems appealing to many people; in fact, to many people, it seems obvious. The core idea of originalism is that when we give meanings to the words of the Constitution, we should use the meanings that the people who adopted those constitutional provisions would have assigned. Those were the people who made the First Amendment, or the Equal Protection Clause, part of the Constitution. According to originalists, it is impermissible—it's a kind of cheating, really—to take the words of the Constitution and give those words a meaning that differs from the understandings of the people who were responsible for including those words in the Constitution in the first place.

There are different kinds of originalism. Some professed originalists will object that the criticisms I am about to make are unfair and turn originalism into a strawperson. I think those originalists actually define "original meaning" in a way that ends up making originalism indistinguishable from a form of living constitutionalism. For now, I'll leave those variations aside; I'll return to them later. There are also relatively subtle refinements in originalism. For example, are the crucial meanings those of the authors of the constitutional provisions, or those of the people who ratified the provisions, or—in the form of originalism that is currently ascendant— simply the meanings that were generally accepted by the public at large at the time the provisions were adopted? These refinements are not important at the moment, because each of these versions of originalism is vulnerable to decisive objections.

The best place to start, in considering the merits and demerits of originalism, is with a particularly rigorous form of originalism, one that is the polar opposite of living constitutionalism. Take, as an example, the Eighth Amendment of the Constitution. It provides that no "cruel and unusual punishments" may be inflicted on people. Of course, the meaning of the word "cruel" (or the phrase "cruel and unusual") is not clear in the way that "January 20" is clear. But we do know that when the Eighth Amendment was adopted in 1791, it was not generally believed that the amendment made the death penalty unconstitutional; in fact, the notion that the Eighth Amendment outlawed the death penalty would have seemed, at the time, to be completely implausible.

According to originalists of the kind I'm discussing, it follows that the death penalty cannot ever be "cruel and unusual." If capital punishment was not understood to violate the Eighth Amendment in 1791, it cannot violate the Eighth Amendment today or at any time in the future. If a constitutional provision was generally understood to permit or forbid something when it was adopted, then it must be understood in the same way today. The Second Amendment says that "the right of the people to keep and bear arms shall not be infringed"; if that phrase, in the context of the amendment, was understood in

1791 to mean that ordinary citizens had a right to have weapons, then today—according to originalists (and according to a majority of the Supreme Court, in a 2008 decision)—the Second Amendment still guarantees ordinary citizens the right to have weapons.

THE ORIGINALISTS' AMERICA

There are many things wrong with originalism. Let's begin with what we would have to give up if we were all to become originalists. There are many principles, deeply embedded in our law, that originalists, if they held their position rigorously, would have to repudiate. The list could be a long one; here is just a sample of what the law would be if originalism were to prevail.

* *Racial segregation of public schools would be constitutional.* In the famous case of *Brown v. Board of Education*, the Supreme Court held that state-imposed racial segregation of schools is unconstitutional under the Equal Protection Clause of the Fourteenth Amendment. But it is clear that when the Fourteenth Amendment was adopted, it was not understood to forbid racial segregation in public schools. At that time, even northern states segregated their schools, if they did not simply exclude African-American children outright. The Congress that proposed the Fourteenth Amendment segregated the schools of the District of Columbia. In fact, while the Fourteenth Amendment was being debated, the Senate galleries themselves were racially segregated. To be sure, some originalists have claimed that *Brown* can be reconciled with originalism, and I will address their arguments later. But even the Supreme Court that decided *Brown*—a Court that had every incentive to invoke the original understandings, since it knew its decision would be attacked as

lawless—essentially conceded that the original understandings did not support its holding, saying, "we cannot turn the clock back to 1868 when the [Fourteenth] Amendment was adopted."

- *The government would be free to discriminate against women.* Since the 1970s, the Supreme Court has held that the Equal Protection Clause of the Fourteenth Amendment limits the power of states to discriminate against women. Even originalists who argue that *Brown* is consistent with original understandings give up when it comes to sex discrimination. At least the Equal Protection Clause was intended to deal with race discrimination of certain kinds, even though it was not understood to outlaw racial segregation in schools. But no one in 1868, when the Fourteenth Amendment was adopted, thought that the amendment outlawed discrimination against women, which was endemic in society and vigorously opposed only by what was regarded as a feminist fringe. Section 2 of the Fourteenth Amendment—a provision, never used, that was designed to penalize states that kept African Americans from voting—actually enshrines sex discrimination, by assuming that the electorate will consist only of men. Feminists Susan B. Anthony and Elizabeth Cady Stanton were furious that the Fourteenth Amendment not only ignored discrimination against women but actually seemed to ratify it, and they actively opposed the Fourteenth Amendment for that reason.

Of course, a lot has happened since 1868. But as far as sex discrimination is concerned, not a lot has happened to the Constitution. The Nineteenth Amendment guaranteed women the right to vote, but that's all. No amendment was ever adopted to guarantee other rights to women. The Equal Rights Amendment, which would have protected women against discrimination, was rejected: Congress proposed it, but too few states ratified it, and it did not become part of the Constitution.

- *The federal government could discriminate against racial minorities (or anyone else) pretty much any time it wanted to.* Even the originalists who think they can justify *Brown* find it difficult to escape this conclusion. The provisions of the Constitution that the Supreme Court relied on in *Brown*, when it declared race and sex discrimination unconstitutional, are in the Fourteenth Amendment—in particular, the clause that says "no state shall... deny to any person within its jurisdiction the equal protection of the laws." But that clause applies only to states—"no state shall... deny"—not to the federal government. The Fourteenth Amendment was adopted in the immediate aftermath of the Civil War, which was fought over the question of states' prerogatives against the federal government. It is inconceivable that the drafters of the Fourteenth Amendment would have sloppily written "state" when they meant "state or federal government."

But on the same day in 1954 that the Supreme Court decided *Brown v. Board of Education*, it also ruled that the federal government could not segregate the public schools in the District of Columbia. The Court has since ruled, without any apparent difficulty, that the same principles that forbid the states to discriminate on the basis of race or sex apply, with equal force and in the same way, to the federal government. As the basis of those rulings, the Supreme Court has relied on a clause in the Fifth Amendment, one that forbids the federal government from denying any person "life, liberty, or property" without "due process of law." The verbal fit between that clause and a principle forbidding discrimination is awkward enough for originalists. But even worse, the Due Process Clause of the Fifth Amendment was adopted in 1791—when race-based slavery was the dominant economic institution in half the country, and the idea that women had equal rights to men was, at best, a radical notion. Yet that is the clause that is used to prohibit the federal government from discriminating. The idea that the original understanding of the Due Process Clause included a principle that the federal government could not discriminate against blacks and women is beyond implausible.

• *The Bill of Rights would not apply to the states.* We are used to thinking that the various provisions of the Bill of Rights apply to "the government." But the Bill of Rights, when it was adopted, applied only to the federal government. Nothing in the U.S. Constitution prohibited the states from abridging religious freedom, subjecting criminal defendants to double jeopardy, conducting unreasonable searches and seizures, or restricting freedom of speech—all things that the Bill of Rights forbids.

When the Fourteenth Amendment was adopted in the wake of the Civil War, there was some discussion about whether that amendment would apply the Bill of Rights to the states. But the language of the Fourteenth Amendment does not explicitly apply the Bill of Rights to the states, and historians differ widely on just how far the Fourteenth Amendment was understood to go in "incorporating" the Bill of Rights. Today, the Bill of Rights—most of it—applies to the states because of a series of Supreme Court decisions. But those decisions have outrun any consensus about the original understandings.

• *States could freely violate the principle of "one person, one vote" in designing their legislatures.* Since 1964, the Supreme Court has insisted that state legislative and congressional districts conform to the principle of one person, one vote. Before the Court's rulings, the legislatures of many states were grotesquely malapportioned. It was common for some districts to have hundreds or even a thousand times as many voters as other districts, even though each district had the same number of representatives. The one person, one vote principle required that each representative in the state legislature represent roughly the same number of people.

This principle is nowhere to be found in the original understandings. The Court relied on the Equal Protection Clause of the Fourteenth Amendment, but that clause, as originally understood, had nothing to do with voting. The Equal Protection Clause was designed to protect recently freed slaves against certain forms of discrimination. But the idea that the ex-slaves could vote was intensely controversial when the Fourteenth Amendment was adopted, and the antidiscrimination provisions of the Fourteenth Amendment were understood not to deal with voting. That was why it was necessary to add, later, the Fifteenth Amendment—which explicitly provides that the right of citizens to vote "shall not be denied or abridged by the United States or by any state on account of race, color, or previous condition of servitude."

Beyond that, malapportioned legislatures were well known to the framers of the original Constitution and to the people who drafted and ratified the Fourteenth Amendment. Neither group gave any indication that it had a constitutional problem with malapportionment. The principle of one person, one vote—very controversial when the Supreme Court first embraced it in 1964—is today hardly controversial at all. But few originalists—I cannot think of any—even try to argue that it follows from the original understandings.

• *Many federal labor, environmental, and consumer protection laws would be unconstitutional.* The size and power of the national government was one of the main subjects of discussion, and controversy, at the Constitutional Convention in 1787. The Constitution establishes a government of limited powers, mostly described in Article I. We do not have a clear picture of the size and power of the federal government that the framers of the Constitution, and the people who ratified it, thought would emerge; no doubt, they disagreed among themselves. But it is clear that the federal government as we know it today is far beyond anything they could have imagined, much less what they thought they were authorizing.

There are many other similar examples. Most of the examples are familiar, and originalists have, to varying degrees, conceded, ducked, or rationalized them. But these are important principles. It is not as if originalism works well for everything except a few esoteric constitutional provisions that don't matter much to anyone. Originalism is inconsistent with principles that are at the core of American constitutional law, and, for the most part, originalists do not claim otherwise.

Justice Antonin Scalia, who is probably the most prominent defender of originalism today, likes to say that he is a "fainthearted originalist," because he is willing to abandon originalism when it leads to implausible results like the ones I described. "I'm an originalist— I'm not a nut," he says. That way of putting it is disarming, but it seems fair to respond: if following a theory consistently would make you a nut, isn't that a problem with the theory?

Less polemically, the problem with fainthearted, or qualified, or sometime originalism is that it gives away most of the qualities that purported to make originalism appealing in the first place. Originalism is supposed to be a bulwark against transient popular sentiment and judges who would impose their own values. But if you're going to say that originalism is only sometimes the right approach, then you have to answer at least two other questions. What principle determines when it is right to abandon originalism? And, once you decide not to be an originalist in a certain category of cases, what do you do instead? The challenge for the fainthearted originalist, the originalist-but-not-a-nut, is to answer these questions without making yourself vulnerable to the same objections that are routinely leveled against living constitutionalism: when push comes to shove, you're just going to do what seems right to you, instead of following the law. And even if the sometime-originalists can rebut those objections, haven't they just turned themselves into sometime-living-constitutionalists? They have acknowledged that the Constitution changes with the times.

The implausible results that originalism produces are actually just symptoms of originalism's deep-seated flaws. There are at least three fundamental problems with originalism.

- On the most practical level, it is often impossible to uncover what the original understandings were: what people thought they were doing when they adopted the various provisions of the Constitution. Discovering how people in the past thought about their world is the task of historians, and there is no reason to think that lawyers and judges are going to be good at doing that kind of history—especially when they are dealing with controversial legal issues that arouse strong sentiments.

- Even if we could uncover the original understandings, we would be faced with the task of translating those understandings so that they address today's problems. The framers or ratifiers of the Constitution had, at best, understandings about *their* world. How do we apply those understandings to *our* world?

- Most fundamental of all, originalists have yet to come to grips with the most obvious and famous issue, one raised by Thomas Jefferson, among others. The world belongs to the living, Jefferson said. Why should we be required to follow decisions made hundreds of years ago by people who are no longer alive? For most of us, the people who made the central decisions about the provisions of the Constitution were not even our ancestors; and it's hard to see why it would matter if they were.

The Problem of Amateur History

Originalism requires us to recover something from the past: the understandings or decisions or meanings of people who adopted the provisions of the U.S. Constitution. That means that judges have to be historians.

In fact, originalist judges have to be better than historians. Historians can choose their subject; if the ideas in circulation at a particular time in history were an incomprehensible mess, a historian can just write her book on a different period, when things made more sense. Originalist judges don't have that luxury. If the case before them is about the Fourth Amendment's ban on unreasonable searches and seizures, then they have to figure out the intellectual history of the Fourth Amendment, however hard that may be. What's more, they have to figure out the intellectual history not just well enough to tell an interesting and illuminating story, as a historian would; judges have to answer the precise question presented by the case before them. It is not enough to try to come to some understanding of the founding generation's ideas about searches of homes and papers, as a historian might. A judge has to decide whether the Fourth Amendment was understood to require, for example, a search warrant before the police looked into a briefcase carried by a person they had arrested.

That kind of fine-grained inquiry into history can be brutally hard. Think about how hard it is even for history that is much more recent. In the 1970s, Congress proposed, and the states nearly ratified, the Equal Rights Amendment to the Constitution, which would have forbidden the federal and state governments from discriminating on the basis of sex. Many of us lived through the debates over the ERA. Do we have a clear idea what the ERA would have required, had it been ratified? Would the ERA have abolished all-girls and all-boys public schools? Would it have required public employers to give women pregnancy leave? Would it have required accommodations for part-time work by women (but not men?) who were caring for children? Those questions were bruited about during the debates over the ERA. Proponents and opponents no doubt postured strategically, in their rhetoric, to try to portray the ERA as either relatively innocuous or as radical and threatening. Different people had different hopes and expectations. No one, I believe, can candidly say that "an understanding" emerged on questions like these. And if we cannot identify clear understandings about something so recent, we have very little chance of accurately uncovering the original understandings of something like the Bill of Rights.

Originalists might respond that the fact that a task is difficult is no reason to refuse to undertake it, and that is a fair point. But the sheer difficulty of uncovering original understandings should give us pause, for several reasons. First, this is a difficult task that is being undertaken by people who have no apparent qualifications for it: judges, most obviously. Judges are lawyers, and there is no reason to think that lawyers will be good at understanding the political culture of a distant century.

Second, and more important, the risk is not just a risk of error, serious as that can be. When historical materials are vague or confused, as they routinely will be, there is an overwhelming temptation for a judge to see in them what the judge wants to see in them. In *District of Columbia v. Heller*, the Supreme Court's 2008 decision about the right to keep and bear arms, the justices divided sharply about the original understanding of the Second Amendment—and the division corresponded neatly to the Court's usual ideological lines. The justices whom one would expect to be sympathetic to the claims of gun owners thought that the original understandings validated their position. The justices whom one would expect to be sympathetic to the claims of cities and states that want to regulate guns thought that the original understandings supported them. No one was surprised at this lineup. Time and again, judges—and academics, too—have found that the original understandings said pretty much what the person examining them wanted them to say. A central criticism of the idea of a living constitution is that it is too manipulable—that a living constitution amounts to substituting judges' own views for the Constitution itself. Originalism, it turns out, is vulnerable to the same criticism.

But what if the original understandings are clear? Everyone agrees, for example, that the Eighth Amendment was not understood, when it was adopted, to forbid capital punishment. Perhaps originalism should be redefined as the view that *clear* original understandings must control. That redefinition would mean that originalism can be used only sometimes. And even in those circumstances, there is still a further problem with originalism, one that can arise no matter how clear the original understandings are. It is the problem of translating those original understandings into principles that can apply to today's issues.

The Problem of Translation

Suppose we know what the original understandings are. Suppose we know for certain, for example, that the Second Amendment was understood to guarantee individual citizens the right to keep firearms in their homes for self-defense. There would be a further, more fundamental problem. The founders (on this hypothesis) wanted to establish this right—in *their* society. They wanted people to have that right in a small, relatively homogeneous, predominantly rural country in which, compared to today, weapons were primitive and the mobility of both people and weapons was limited.

It does not follow that the founders would want the same thing for *our* society. It is possible that, if they had been able to envision the twenty-first century, they would have said that firearms could be extensively regulated. Of course, we don't know that for sure; it's just speculation. But that's the point.

These arguments might seem like too-clever debater's points, but they are not. This basic problem—what do you do when circumstances change?—can occur whenever someone has an obligation to follow instructions given by another person and cannot communicate with the person who gave the instructions. Take a simple example: a military commander's orders to a subordinate. The subordinate has a duty to follow the orders. But what if circumstances change in a crucial way after the subordinate receives the orders, and communications are cut off? (We cannot, after all, communicate with the framers or ratifiers of the Constitution.) The subordinate has to make a judgment about whether the commander intended the orders to be followed literally even in the changed circumstances. If the answer is that the commander probably did not foresee these circumstances and therefore, in that sense, did not so intend, the subordinate then has to decide, perhaps, on what course of action most closely corresponds to the commander's intentions. When the orders were given recently, and the change in circumstances was not too dramatic, and the commander and subordinate are similar in their general views, then these questions might have reasonably clear answers. But when the commanders lived in the late eighteenth or mid-nineteenth century, and the subordinate has to act in the twenty-first century, it is delusive to think that these questions can be answered with any confidence.

This kind of problem arises over and over in constitutional interpretation. The Constitution gives Congress the power to regulate "Commerce...among the several States." Today, that provision is interpreted to authorize Congress to regulate a wide range of conduct that occurs within states, on the theory that the intrastate conduct has some connection to other states or to interstate commerce. Is that interpretation inconsistent with the original understandings? It's quite clear that, when the founders adopted the Commerce Clause, they did not understand themselves to be authorizing such sweeping federal regulatory power.

But that was their understanding about how the Commerce Clause would operate in their society and economy. Our society and economy are incomparably more complex and interconnected. What could have been the understanding, in 1787, about what Congress's Commerce Clause power should be in a society that looks like ours today, with today's means of transportation and communication, and today's institutions of trade and finance? A society like ours would have been, literally, almost inconceivable at that time. Even if it had been conceivable, why would people who were intensely engaged in resolving their own difficult constitutional issues have tried to formulate a view about such a futuristic question? And if some people had, remarkably, formulated such a view, what is the chance that a general understanding existed?

Asking about the original understanding of how the Second Amendment or the Commerce Clause would apply to twenty-first-century America would be a little like asking: what was the 1970s understanding of how the ERA would apply to a world in which, say, babies could be born without women going through pregnancy, and men and women shared child-care duties equally? It's an unanswerable question: of course there was no generally shared understanding about how the ERA would apply in such an imaginary world. Asking how the ERA would apply in that world would be, at best, an abstract, academic question that would produce—well, among most people, it would produce an impatient shrug or an indulgent smile. The idea that there was an understanding about the correct answer to this question is absurd. But originalism requires us to pretend that, in the past, there were just those kinds of understandings.

Jefferson's Problem

The most fundamental problem with originalism is the one that Thomas Jefferson, among others, identified in the earliest days of the Constitution. "The earth belongs... to the living," Jefferson wrote to James Madison in 1789. One generation cannot bind another: "We seem not to have perceived that, by the law of nature, one generation is to another as one independent nation is to another." To paraphrase (and update) Jefferson's contemporary Noah Webster, twenty-first-century Americans have infinitely more in common with, say, the present-day residents of New Zealand—demographically, morally, culturally, and in our historical experiences—than we do with the people who gave us the Constitution more than 200 years ago. But it would be bizarre to suggest that we should let the people of New Zealand decide fundamental questions about our law. Why do we submit to the decisions of the much more distant and alien founders?

I believe there are answers to these questions, but the answers do not support originalism—and I do not believe that the originalists have given a good answer. It is not sufficient to say, as many do, that the Constitution is law. Of course the Constitution is law, but declaring that it is law does not determine how it should be interpreted. Nor is it a good answer to say that we are engaged in a multigenerational project with our forebears who brought forth the Constitution. In some sense that is true, too, but it does not follow that we must adhere to our forebears' understandings. First we have to determine the nature of the multigenerational project. It is also not satisfactory, in my view, to say (as many do) that we must show "fidelity" to the founding generations. I think we should be uncomfortable, in general, with the invocation of quasi-religious notions like fidelity in a diverse society like ours, where there is no orthodoxy and people may choose to give fidelity to any of a countless number of cultural and religious traditions. But in any event, talk of "fidelity" just raises the question of what fidelity requires. It may require adapting the Constitution to modern circumstances, à la the living Constitution, rather than adhering to the original understandings.

Jefferson's argument is, I think, ultimately fatal to originalism, at least if originalism is offered as a general approach to interpreting the U.S. Constitution. But it is important not to be facile about this. There is a sense in which Jefferson's claim proves too much. Everyone—originalist or not—believes that the text of the Constitution is law. No one would cast aside the Constitution altogether. Why does each state get two senators, regardless of population? The answer is that this is the arrangement that the framers made more than 200 years ago. To that extent, no one is a thoroughgoing Jeffersonian. In chapter 5, I will propose a way in which we might adhere to the text of the Constitution—as, to some degree, everyone does—without encountering Jefferson's objection. But for now, the important point is that originalists—who believe that the understandings of people long dead should govern, in principle, every aspect of constitutional law—have not given Jefferson a satisfactory answer.

MODERATE ORIGINALISM

I have criticized a particularly rigorous form of originalism, one that insists that the original understandings of constitutional provisions provide answers to every dispute about what the Constitution requires. Many people who call themselves originalists do not accept originalism in this form. Perhaps the most common alternative form of originalism says that what is binding is not the specific original understandings but instead the principles that the framers or ratifiers of the Constitution were understood to be establishing.

Take, for example, *Brown v. Board of Education*, the school segregation case. As I said earlier, it is quite clear that the Fourteenth Amendment, when it was adopted, was not understood to forbid school segregation. But according to the moderate originalists (as I'll call them), that is beside the point. The important thing about the original understandings is not the specific outcomes that the drafters and ratifiers envisioned. What is important is that the Fourteenth Amendment was understood, at the time, to be establishing a principle of racial equality. The fact that the principle was understood to be consistent with segregated schools is neither here nor there. If we determine, today, that segregation is *not* consistent with racial equality, we can forbid segregation without violating the original understandings—because we are faithfully adhering to the principle of racial equality that the Fourteenth Amendment embodies. We have no obligation to adhere to the specific outcomes that the earlier generations envisioned, so long as we follow their principles.

This kind of moderate originalism is very popular, and it takes a variety of forms—for example, that we are obligated to follow the original "meanings" but not the original "applications." But the key point about this kind of moderate originalism is that it changes the level of generality at which the original understandings are described. Instead of saying that the original understanding is that "school segregation is acceptable," we should say that the original understanding is that "racial equality is required." Moderate originalism of this kind can easily accommodate the examples I gave earlier of settled constitutional rules that are inconsistent with rigorous originalism. Once the original understandings are described at a certain level of generality—at the level of principle rather than specific outcomes—all of those rules (*Brown*; one person, one vote; and so on) are consistent with the original understandings.

The problem with this kind of moderate originalism is that it can justify anything. Once we say that we are bound only by the principle, rather than by the specific outcomes, that the founders envisioned, we can always make the principle abstract enough to justify any result we want to reach.

The Eighth Amendment, for example, forbids "cruel and unusual punishments" but was understood, when it was adopted, not to outlaw the death penalty. For rigorous originalists, that original understanding about the death penalty is decisive. Moderate originalists, though, might say that the proper description of the original understanding is the principle that "cruel punishments are forbidden." Given that original understanding, it is up to us, today, to decide whether the death penalty is cruel. Judges can disagree with the founders about whether the death penalty is constitutional but still act in a way that is consistent with the original understandings, because they are adhering to the principle that cruel punishments are unconstitutional.

But now judges are free to declare any punishment unconstitutional, as long as they conclude that it is cruel. If the idea behind originalism is to provide some limit on what judges can do (or on what can be done by other constitutional interpreters, for example in the executive branch), moderate originalism fails. Judges are free to do what they want; they just have to derive from some constitutional provision a "principle" that supports them. Given the abstract and general language of the text of the Constitution, that will seldom be much of an obstacle.

School segregation is another example. Moderate originalists admit that, when the Fourteenth Amendment was adopted, the general understanding was that school segregation was constitutional;

they justify *Brown* by saying that, for purposes of constitutional interpretation, the original understanding should be characterized not at that level of specificity but at the level of the principle of racial equality. The problem is: why stop there, with *racial* equality? Why not say that the original understanding was that equality should be guaranteed for all minorities who are oppressed in the way that the newly freed slaves were being oppressed? That is not a false description of the original understanding, even if the view, back then, was that only the newly freed slaves fell into that category. (In fact, the framers of the Fourteenth Amendment probably did think that other groups fell into that category.) Once we treat "equality for oppressed minorities" as the true original understanding, the courts, acting consistently with (moderate) originalism, are free to strike down, say, laws that discriminate against women or gays—or, for that matter, laws that discriminate against landlords—if the judges think that women or gays or landlords are the appropriate kind of oppressed minority. We have no reason to suppose that the drafters and ratifiers of the Fourteenth Amendment thought that women or gays or landlords fell into the same category as African Americans. But under moderate originalism, we are not bound by their views on who fell into that category, any more than we are bound by their view that segregation is consistent with racial equality.

In a word, the problem with moderate originalism is that, once we move away from the specific outcomes that were envisioned, the choice of a level of generality at which to describe the original understandings is an arbitrary choice. That's not to say that moderate originalism is necessarily disingenuous, or anything of that kind. It is perfectly fine to try to identify ways in which we are maintaining continuity with the principles of earlier generations, even while we disagree with the way those principles are applied. The point is that this form of originalism does not do what originalism is supposed to do. It does not confine judges or other constitutional interpreters. It leaves them free to decide cases based mostly on their own values. (Is capital punishment cruel? Is the treatment of gays, today, sufficiently similar to the treatment of blacks in the South after the Civil War?) Originalism, so understood, cannot even claim the one advantage it purports to have over living constitutionalism.

WHY IS ORIGINALISM APPEALING?

None of these criticisms of originalism is new; most of them, in one form or another, have been around for decades. Today, we think of originalism as an approach that conservatives favor, because for the last generation the most prominent defenders of originalism have been conservatives. But in the 1940s, '50s, and '60s, the most prominent originalist was Justice Black, who would, on most issues, certainly be considered a liberal—and whose influence on the law far surpassed the influence of today's conservative originalists. Justice Black's conservative critics made many of the same points against his originalism that today's anti-originalists make against conservative originalists.

The real puzzle about originalism is how it survives in the face of repeated and telling criticism. There are, I think, at least three reasons. The first is that there is something natural about originalism. Constitutional law is supposed to consist in the interpretation of a written text. Routinely, when we interpret a text, we think about how the authors of the text understood the words they used. That would usually be true of a personal letter, for example, or of a commanding officer's order in the military analogy I gave earlier. (Literary interpretation presents separate issues, but there is at least a prominent school of literary criticism that takes the view that the authors' understandings are controlling.) Why shouldn't this be true of the Constitution?

The answer is that it is true of a constitution—sometimes. If a constitutional provision has been enacted recently, the understandings should control. Suppose that the Constitution were amended to allow "voluntary prayer" in public schools, and the generally shared understanding was that the amendment authorized officially prescribed prayers, led by a teacher; the prayers would be considered voluntary as long as students could remain silent or leave the classroom. If that was the general understanding, then in the immediate aftermath of such an amendment, it would, in my view, be an incorrect interpretation of the Constitution to hold that the amendment had any other meaning. It would be wrong, for example, to say that teacher-led prayer was necessarily not "voluntary" and therefore was not authorized.

But the understandings are often not so clear. More important, even if they are clear, as time passes, the reasons for adhering to the original understandings begin to fade. The fundamental flaws of originalism that I discussed earlier begin to appear. It becomes difficult to know how to apply the original understandings to new circumstances. And, in particular, Jefferson's problem asserts itself.

All of the constitutional provisions that give rise to today's controversies are old. The most controversial are more than a century old. Originalism is no longer a natural way to interpret those provisions. And we do not, in fact, interpret the Constitution in the way demanded by rigorous originalism. That is evident from the many examples I gave earlier of settled constitutional principles that are inconsistent with original understandings; and in the later chapters of this book, I will show in detail that American constitutional law is the product of an evolutionary form of living constitutionalism, not of originalism.

The second reason that originalism persists, despite the force of the criticisms, is that originalism is not actually a way of interpreting the Constitution. It is a rhetorical trope. People defend a position—a position that they hold for some other reason—by attributing it to the founders. Originalism is a particularly valuable rhetorical device for people who are trying to overturn part of the established legal order. If current law is against you, you have to appeal to something—so you invoke the founders. Justice Black was a leading critic of the constitutional order that he inherited, one that protected economic liberties more vigorously than freedom of speech or the rights of disadvantaged minorities. He invoked the founders as part of his (highly successful) crusade against that old order. A generation later, conservatives reacted against what they saw as the excesses of the Supreme Court led by Chief Justice Earl Warren; now, it was their turn to invoke the founders.

The third reason originalism persists is that, for all its flaws, it has no established competitor. A proponent of the living Constitution is open to the withering objections I described at the outset: that the living Constitution is infinitely flexible and has no content other than the views of the person who is doing the interpreting. Living constitutionalism means that the restraints are off, and anything goes.

In the remaining chapters, I will describe a kind of living constitutionalism that is not open to these objections—and that, unlike originalism, corresponds to the way in which American constitutional law actually develops.

CHAPTER TWO

The Common Law

PICK UP A Supreme Court opinion in a constitutional case, at random. Look at how the justices justify the result they reach. Here is a prediction: the text of the Constitution will play, at most, a ceremonial role. Most of the real work will be done by the Court's analysis of its previous decisions. The opinion may begin with a quotation from the text. "The Fourth Amendment provides...," the opinion might say. Then, having been dutifully acknowledged, the text bows out. The next line will begin with "We"—meaning the Supreme Court—"have interpreted the Amendment to require..." And there will follow a detailed, careful account of the Court's precedents.

Where the precedents leave off, or are unclear or ambiguous, the opinion will make arguments about fairness or good policy: why one result makes more sense than another, why a different ruling would be harmful to some important social interest. The original understandings play a role only occasionally, and usually they are makeweights, or the Court admits that they are inconclusive. There are exceptions, like *Heller*, the 2008 decision about the Second Amendment right to bear arms, in which the original understandings took center stage. But cases like that are rare—and the opinions in that case, which purported to analyze the text and the original understandings, actually seem to be motivated more by the justices' respective policy views about gun control.

Advocates know what actually moves the Court. Briefs are filled with analysis of the precedents and arguments about which result makes sense as a matter of policy or fairness. Oral arguments in the Court work the same way. The text of the Constitution hardly ever gets mentioned. It is the unusual case in which the original understandings get much attention. In constitutional cases, the discussion at oral argument will be about the Court's previous decisions and, often, hypothetical questions designed to test whether a particular interpretation will lead to results that are implausible as a matter of common sense.

The contrast between constitutional law and the interpretation of statutes is particularly revealing. When a case concerns the interpretation of a statute, the briefs, the oral arguments, and the opinions will usually focus on the precise words of the statute. But when a case involves the Constitution, the text routinely gets no attention. On a day-to-day basis, American constitutional law is about precedents, and when the precedents leave off, it is about commonsense notions of fairness and good policy.

What's going on here? Don't we have a Constitution? We do, but if you think the Constitution is just the document that is under glass in the National Archives, you will not begin to understand American constitutional law. The written Constitution is a short document that has been amended only a handful of times. By comparison, the United States has over two centuries of experience grappling with the fundamental issues—constitutional issues—that arise in a large, complex, diverse, changing society. The lessons we have learned in grappling with those issues only sometimes make their way into the text of the Constitution by way of amendments, and even then the amendments often occur only after the law has already changed. But those lessons are routinely embodied in the cases that the Supreme Court decides and also, importantly, in the traditions and understandings that have developed outside the courts. Those precedents, traditions, and understandings form an indispensable part of what might be called our small-*c* constitution: the constitution as it actually operates, in practice. That small-*c* constitution—along with the written Constitution in the archives—is our living Constitution.

In chapters 3 and 4, I will describe how two of the most important doctrines in American constitutional law—the protection of freedom of speech, associated with the First Amendment, and the historic decision in *Brown v. Board of Education*, which declared racial segregation to be unconstitutional—came about not through the careful reading of the text, and not through adherence to the original understandings, but through the evolution of precedents. But my first task is to explain what it means to say that the living Constitution develops through the accumulation and evolution of precedents, shaped to some degree by notions of fairness and good policy.

In particular, it is important to explain how *law* can develop in that evolutionary way. That kind of development, characteristic of our living Constitution, is often messy. It is not like solving a math problem; it is not algorithmic. It involves the exercise of judgment. It explicitly involves arguments and considerations that aren't narrowly or distinctively legal, like judgments about fairness and good policy. As a result, it's easy to say that living constitutionalism of that kind is not law, because law is supposed to be neat, clean, open and shut.

But the kind of development I describe—in which precedents evolve, shaped by notions of fairness and good policy—is one of the oldest and most effective kinds of law. It is the common law, which has been around for centuries, long before there was a written U.S. Constitution. The basic principles of the most important areas of private law—property, torts, and contracts—were developed not by legislation but by the common law, by the accumulation of precedents. The common law was the dominant form of law in the United States (and in the United Kingdom) until the twentieth century, and it remains important in many areas to this day.

The principal concern about living constitutionalism is that it amounts to giving a blank check to judges and other interpreters. But the common law has, for centuries, restrained judges; in fact, it restrains judges more effectively than originalism does. The common law approach is also more justifiable than originalism. And the common law approach provides a far better understanding of what our constitutional law actually is.

THE TWO TRADITIONS

There are, broadly speaking, two competing accounts of how something gets to be law. One account—probably the one that comes most easily to mind—sees law as, essentially, an order from a boss. The "boss" need not be a dictator; it can be a democratically elected legislature. According to this theory, the law is binding on us because the person or entity that commanded it had the authority to issue such a binding command either, say, because of the divine right of kings, or—the modern version—because of the legitimacy of democratic rule. But the law is, in the final analysis, an authoritative command from someone. So if you want to determine what the law is, you examine what the boss, the sovereign, did: the words the sovereign used, evidence of the sovereign's intentions, and so on.

Originalism is a version of this approach. As originalists see it, the Constitution is law because it was ratified by "the People," either in the late 1700s or when the various amendments were adopted. Anything the people did not ratify isn't the law. If we want to determine what the Constitution requires, we have to examine what the people did: what words they adopted, and what they understood themselves to be doing when they adopted those provisions. And we have to stop there. Once we look beyond the text and the original understandings, we're no longer looking for law; we're doing something else, like reading our own values into the law.

The command theory, though, isn't the only way to think about law. The common law approach is the great competitor of the command theory, in a competition that has gone on for centuries. The common law approach has deep roots, medieval roots, according to some accounts. The early common lawyers saw the common law as a species of custom. The law was a particular set of customs, and it emerged in the way that customs often emerge in a society. It would make no sense to ask who was the sovereign who commanded that a certain custom prevail, or when, precisely, a particular custom became established. Customs do not have identifiable origins like that. Legal systems are now too complex and esoteric to be regarded as society-wide customs. But still, on the common law view, the law can be like a custom in important ways. It can develop over time, not at a single moment; it can be the evolutionary product of many people, in many generations. There does not have to be one entity who commanded the law in a discrete act at a particular time.

Similarly, according to the common law view, the authority of the law comes not from the fact that some entity has the right, democratic or otherwise, to rule. It comes instead from the law's evolutionary origins and its general acceptability to successive generations. Legal rules that have been worked out over an extended period can claim obedience for that reason alone. For the same reason, according to the common law approach, you cannot determine the content of the law by examining a single authoritative text or the intentions of a single entity. The content of the law is determined by the evolutionary process that produced it. Present-day interpreters may contribute to the evolution—but only by continuing the evolution, not by ignoring what exists and starting anew.

Characteristically, the law emerges from this evolutionary process through the development of a body of precedents. A judge who is faced with a difficult issue looks to how earlier courts decided that issue, or similar issues. The judge starts by assuming that she will do the same thing in the case before her that the earlier court did in similar cases. Sometimes—almost always, in fact—the precedents will be clear, and there will be no room for reasonable disagreement about what the precedents dictate. But sometimes, the earlier cases will not dictate a result. The earlier cases may not resemble the present case closely enough. Or there may be earlier cases that point in different directions, suggesting opposite outcomes in the case before the judge. Then the judge has to decide what to do.

At that point—when the precedents are not clear—a variety of technical issues can enter into the picture. But often, when the precedents are not clear, the judge will decide the case before her on the basis of her views about which decision will be more fair or is more in keeping with good social policy. This is a well-established aspect of the common law: it is not simply a matter of following precedent. There is a legitimate role for judgments about things like fairness and social policy.

It is important not to exaggerate (nor to understate) how large a role these kinds of judgments play in a common law system.

Benjamin Cardozo, one of the greatest American common law judges, put it this way:

> The final cause of law is the welfare of society. The rule that misses its aim cannot permanently justify its existence.... [But] I do not mean, of course, that judges are commissioned to set aside existing rules at pleasure in favor of any other set of rules which they may hold to be expedient or wise. I mean that when they are called upon to say how far existing rules are to be extended or restricted, they must let the welfare of society fix the path, its direction and its distance.

In any well-functioning legal system, most potential cases do not even get to court, because the law is so clear that people do not dispute it, and that is true of common law systems too. Even in the small minority of cases in which the law is disputed, the correct answer will sometimes be clear. And—perhaps the most important point—even when the outcome is not clear, and arguments about fairness or good policy come into play, the precedents will usually limit the possible outcomes that a judge can reach.

For example, in a case in which a person who was injured by a defective car sues the manufacturer—I'll discuss a famous common law case of this kind in a later chapter—the precedents might leave open the question whether the victim has to show that the manufacturer was careless or can instead recover damages even if the manufacturer took reasonable precautions. The judge might decide between those two options based on her ideas about good policy. But that is different from the judge simply enacting her policy views, because the precedents might (and, in this case, do) foreclose a wide range of more extreme outcomes, however appealing those outcomes might be to the judge. No judge could plausibly rule that the victim can never recover, or can recover only if the manufacturer deliberately put a defective car on the market, or (on the other end of the spectrum) that the victim can recover from the manufacturer for any accident, even if the car was in good shape. In other words, even where the precedents are not decisive, and judgments about fairness or social policy come into play, they come into play only in the narrow range left open by the precedents.

Judgments of policy and fairness can come into play in the common law in another way as well. The working presumption in a common law system is that judges should follow precedent. But this is not an inflexible rule; in a common law system, judges sometimes may overrule precedents. When can a judge properly do that? The answer is complex—I will describe one such example in chapter 4—but there is no doubt that judgments about fairness and social policy enter into the picture, although again in a limited way.

ATTITUDES, NOT ALGORITHMS

This description might seem to make the common law a vague and open-ended system that leaves too much up for grabs—precisely the kinds of criticisms often directed at the idea of a living constitution. When, exactly, can a case be distinguished from an earlier precedent? What are the rules for deciding between conflicting precedents? What are the rules about overturning precedents?

For the most part, there are no clear, definitive rules in a common law system. The common law is, as I said, not algorithmic. The better way to think about the common law is that it is governed by a set of attitudes: attitudes of humility and cautious empiricism. These attitudes, taken together, make up a kind of ideology of the common law. It's an ideology that was systematically elaborated by some of the great common law judges of early modern England. The most famous exponent of this ideology was the British statesman Edmund Burke, who wrote in the late eighteenth century. Burke, a classic conservative, wrote about politics and society generally, not specifically about the law. But he took the common law as his model for how society at large should change, and he explained (although that is not quite the right word for Burke's unsystematic writing) the underpinnings of that view.

The first attitude at the foundation of the common law is humility about the power of individual human reason. It is a bad idea to try to resolve a problem on your own, without referring to the collective wisdom of other people who have tried to solve the same problem. That is why it makes sense to follow precedent, especially if the precedents are clear and have been established for a long time. "We are afraid to put men to live and trade each on his own stock of reason," Burke said, "because we suspect that this stock in each man is small, and that the individuals would do better to avail themselves of the general bank and capital of nations." The accumulated precedents are "the general bank and capital." It is an act of intellectual hubris to think that you know better than that accumulated wisdom.

The second attitude is an inclination to ask "what has worked in practice?" It is a distrust of abstractions when those abstractions call for casting aside arrangements that have been satisfactory in practice, even if the arrangements cannot be fully justified in abstract terms. The world is a complicated place; no body of theory can fully account for it. If a practice or an institution has survived and seems to work well, those are good reasons to preserve it; that practice probably embodies a kind of rough common sense, based in experience, that cannot be captured in theoretical abstractions. To quote Burke again: "The science of government being...so practical in itself, and intended for such practical purposes, a matter which requires experience, and even more experience than any person can gain in his whole life,... it is with infinite caution that any man ought to venture upon pulling down an edifice, which has answered in any tolerable degree for ages the common purposes of society."

The evolution of attitudes toward affirmative action in the United States may be an example of the triumph of this kind of Burkean conservatism. When affirmative action first became a political and constitutional issue, the practice of favoring minority groups was roundly attacked, and not just by political conservatives. The attack was abstract: society should be color-blind. Racial classifications have no place in a nation committed to equality. People should be judged on merit, not on race. Some of us believe that those arguments are simply mistaken even in their own abstract terms, but those arguments were, and are, widely accepted.

Over time, though, affirmative action came to be accepted in institutions throughout American society: corporations, professions, government agencies, universities, the military. The people who implemented affirmative action in these settings did so, in many instances, not because they were convinced that the abstract criticisms of affirmative action were wrong, but rather because affirmative action worked: a diverse workforce (or student body, or officer corps) was a better workforce, and the only way to get a diverse workforce was to take race into account in hiring and promotions. Today, more than three decades after the first legal challenges to affirmative action, it seems fair to say that affirmative action is entrenched in many American institutions, even though there is no consensus on its abstract justification, no generally agreed-upon answer to the assertion that our society should be color-blind. The only generally accepted answer seems to be the Burkean one: the world is more complicated than that, and affirmative action works.

ORIGINALISM, THE COMMON LAW, AND CANDOR

Originalism's trump card—the principal reason it is taken seriously, despite its manifold and repeatedly identified weaknesses—is the seeming lack of a plausible opponent. Living constitutionalism seems too vague, too manipulable.

But if the living Constitution is a common law constitution, then originalism can no longer claim to be the only game in town. The common law has been around for centuries. In nonconstitutional areas, it has a long track record of limiting judges' discretion and guiding the behavior of individuals. And while the common law does not always provide crystal-clear answers, it is false to say that a common law system, based on precedent, is endlessly manipulable.

A common law approach is superior to originalism in at least four ways.

• The common law approach is more workable. Originalism requires judges and lawyers to be historians. The common law approach requires judges and lawyers to be, well, judges and lawyers. Reasoning from precedent, with occasional resort to basic notions of fairness and good policy, is what judges and lawyers do. They have done it for a long time in the nonconstitutional areas that are governed by the common law.

• The common law approach is more justifiable. The common law ideology gives a plausible explanation for why we should follow precedent. One might disagree, to a greater or lesser extent, with that ideology. Perhaps abstract reason is better than Burke allows; perhaps we should be more willing to make changes based on our theoretical constructions. Sometimes, the past is not a storehouse of wisdom; it might be the product of sheer happenstance or, worse, accumulated injustice. But there is unquestionably something to the

Burkean arguments. And to the extent that those arguments are exaggerated, the common law approach has enough flexibility to allow a greater role for abstract ideas of fairness and good policy and a smaller role for precedent.

Originalists, by contrast, do not have an answer to Jefferson's question: why should we allow people who lived long ago, in a different world, to decide fundamental questions about our government and society today? Originalists do not draw on the accumulated wisdom of previous generations in the way that the common law does; only a fainthearted originalist pays any attention to anything that happened after a constitutional provision was adopted. For an originalist, the command was issued at that point—when a provision became part of the Constitution—and our unequivocal obligation is to follow that command. But why? It is one thing to be commanded by a legislature we elected last year. It is quite another to be commanded by the people who assembled in the Constitutional Convention and the state ratifying conventions in the late eighteenth century.

• The common law approach is what we actually do. Originalists' America—in which states can segregate schools, the federal government can discriminate against anybody, any government can discriminate against women, state legislatures can be malapportioned, states needn't comply with most of the Bill of Rights, and Social Security is unconstitutional—doesn't look much like the country we inhabit. In controversial areas at least—leaving aside such things as the length of the president's term of office—the governing principles of constitutional law are the product of precedents, not of the text or the original understandings. And in the actual practice of constitutional law, precedents and arguments about fairness and social policy are dominant.

• The common law approach is more candid. This is an important and easily underrated virtue of the common law approach, especially compared to originalism. The common law approach explicitly envisions that judges will be influenced by their own views about fairness and social policy. Common law judges have operated that way for centuries. This doesn't mean that judges can do what they want. Judgments of that kind can operate only in limited ways: in the area left open by precedent, or in the circumstances in which it is appropriate to overrule a precedent. But because it is legitimate to make judgments about fairness and policy, in a common law system those judgments can be openly avowed and defended—and therefore can be openly criticized.

Originalism is different. An originalist claims to be following orders. An originalist cannot be influenced by her own judgments about fairness or social policy; to allow that kind of influence is, for an originalist, a lawless act of usurpation. (I'm leaving aside cases in which the original understanding was that judges were free to do what they thought best; in those instances, originalism and living constitutionalism may converge in practice.) An originalist has to insist that she is just enforcing the original understanding of the Second Amendment, or the Free Exercise Clause of the First Amendment, and that her own views about gun control or religious liberty have nothing whatever to do with her decision.

That is an invitation to be disingenuous. Originalism, as applied to the controversial provisions of the U.S. Constitution, is shot through with indeterminacy—a result of the problems I discussed earlier, the problems of ascertaining the original understandings and of translating those understandings once they've been ascertained. In the face of that indeterminacy, it will be difficult for any judge to sideline his strongly held views about the issue. But originalism forbids the judge from putting those views on the table and openly defending them. Instead, the judge's views have to be attributed to the framers, and the debate has to proceed in pretend-historical terms, instead of in terms of what is, more than likely, actually determining the outcome.

Having said all that, though, the proof is in the pudding, and the common law Constitution—the living Constitution—cannot be effectively defended until we see it in operation. In the next two chapters, I will show how two of the most impressive achievements of American constitutional law are the product not of the text or the original understandings, but of the common law, the living Constitution.

IS THE COMMON LAW UNDEMOCRATIC?

Historically, the common law has been a source of law in areas like contracts, torts, property, and criminal law. Common law decisions in these areas can be overturned by legislatures (generally by state legislatures, because these are areas of state law). A decision about the meaning of the Constitution, by contrast, cannot be reversed by Congress or a state legislature; it can only be undone if the courts change course, or if the Constitution is formally amended, an exceptionally difficult process.

Some critics of the common law approach to constitutional interpretation have argued that this is a fatal defect in that approach. The common law approach is acceptable, they say, only when, as has historically been the case, judicial decisions can be changed by the simple passage of a law. Then the people's representatives can correct the courts when the courts go astray. But when the courts are interpreting the Constitution, their decisions cannot be corrected in that way, and consequently—the critics say—the common law approach to constitutional interpretation is fundamentally, and unacceptably, antidemocratic.

There is certainly something undemocratic, in a sense, about the U.S. constitutional system. But it is not the common law approach that makes our system undemocratic. What makes our system undemocratic is judicial review: the practice of allowing the courts to have the last word on most issues of constitutional law. And, at a deeper level, the Constitution itself is in some ways undemocratic. It will sometimes prevent the majority from having its way if, for example, the majority wants to suppress political dissent or discriminate against racial minorities. While there is a persistent and powerful strand of thought that condemns judicial review, most of us think that these "undemocratic" features of our system are a good thing.

In a constitutional system with judicial review, like ours, the courts have to have a way of resolving disputes over constitutional issues. That is where the common law approach comes into the picture. The common law is not intrinsically democratic or undemocratic; it is a way of resolving legal issues. The fact that the common law approach developed in connection with nonconstitutional legal issues—issues on which legislatures, not courts, have the last word—does not mean that the common law approach has to be limited to those issues. The common law approach has the virtues I have described: it requires humility and commonsense empiricism, it allows for the candid exercise of judgment but only within narrow bounds, and it has a centuries-long track record of limiting judges. All of these are good reasons to use the common law approach when constitutional questions arise, too.

This point—that there is nothing intrinsically antidemocratic about the common law approach—can be seen in another way as well. Other institutions, besides courts, can use a common law approach to making decisions. Edmund Burke's argument was precisely that the common law should be a model for all of a society's institutions. Closer to home, when Congress or the executive branch has the last word on constitutional issues in the United States—as those branches sometimes do—they often use a precedent-based, common law approach. The Office of Legal Counsel in the Department of Justice, which has responsibility for resolving constitutional issues within the executive branch, treats its own previous decisions in roughly the same way that the Supreme Court treats its precedents. When Congress was considering whether to impeach and remove President Bill Clinton, a principal source of law was the precedent of the near-impeachment of President Richard Nixon. Private organizations also often use a precedent-based approach, comparable to the common law: when faced with an issue, they consider what they did previously in similar circumstances and whether it seemed to work or not.

It is, therefore, easy to imagine common law constitutionalism in a system without judicial review. Constitutional decisions—whether a law infringed on constitutional rights to freedom of speech, or denied equal protection, or permitted unreasonable searches and seizures—would be made not by courts but by members of Congress conscientiously applying earlier decisions and understandings. Congress and the executive branch do often act this way, when (as in the case of impeachment) they have the last word, or when, even though the courts will have the last word, the elected officials believe that there is a constitutional issue that they should take seriously. Is this an undemocratic way to proceed? Only to the extent that, as I said earlier, the Constitution itself is undemocratic. Nothing about the common law approach makes common law constitutionalism undemocratic.

The argument that the common law approach is undemocratic, especially when made by originalists, relies on a kind of sleight of hand. Originalism, its proponents say, carries out the will of the people who adopted the Constitution, and is therefore democratic. Common law constitutionalism, by contrast, reflects the will of the judges—or so the originalists say—and that is why it is undemocratic. But there are many things wrong with this argument. The people who adopted the Constitution are no longer with us, and, as Jefferson and others have said, it is hard to see why it is "democratic" to follow the will of people who lived so long ago. Apart from that, originalist judges have to decide what those people's will was about issues that the people could not have anticipated—and that leaves plenty of room for undemocratic rule by judges. And, in any event, we do not have a purely democratic system. We have a system in which the courts, applying the Constitution, sometimes prevent the majority from having its way. The question is, when should the courts do that? The common law approach gives us a way to answer that question—a way that makes sense in the abstract and that conforms to how our system has worked in practice.

CHAPTER THREE

Freedom of Speech
and the Living Constitution

THE FIRST AMENDMENT to the U.S. Constitution is probably the most celebrated text in all of American law. With the possible exception of the Fifth Amendment, which may be more notorious than famous, no other provision of the Constitution is as familiar to nonlawyers. The American system of freedom of expression—the principles that protect freedom of speech in the United States—is correspondingly impressive, in several respects. It is an elaborate set of principles that provides relatively clear guidance to governments, to media firms, and to others who have to decide in advance what people have a right to say. It has helped to foster a culture of political and artistic expression that is exceptionally robust by historical and even contemporary standards.

The First Amendment has also come to occupy a special place in American constitutional law. For most of the twentieth century, the central issue in constitutional law was whether the courts should be "activist" in striking down laws that they believed to be inconsistent with the Constitution or should instead be deferential and uphold laws of questionable constitutionality. ("Judicial activism" is a term of many meanings—sometimes, it is just an epithet—but one relatively clear meaning is the willingness to declare laws unconstitutional, as opposed to giving the benefit of every doubt to Congress or to the state legislature that enacted the law.) Over the course of the twentieth century, liberals and conservatives changed sides on this issue. Roughly speaking, liberals urged restraint when activist conservatives struck down laws that regulated business; conservatives urged restraint when liberals struck down laws that, they believed, treated disadvantaged minorities unfairly. But by the late decades of the twentieth century, essentially everyone was in favor of activism when it came to the First Amendment. The argument for judicial restraint in the enforcement of the First Amendment—a prominent position in the 1940s, '50s, '60s, and '70s—had essentially no adherents by 2000.

In all of these senses, the First Amendment—that is, the principles protecting free speech—has been a tremendous success story in American constitutional law. But where did these successful principles come from? They did not come from the text of the Constitution. The First Amendment was part of the Constitution for a century and a half before the central principles of the American regime of free speech, as we now know it, became established in the law. Nor did those principles come from the original understandings. There is a natural tendency to attribute to the framers of the Constitution great foresight and enlightened views about freedom of expression (as well as other subjects), but the actual views of the drafters and ratifiers of the First Amendment are in many ways unclear. To the extent that we can determine the views of those people, they did not think they were establishing a system of freedom of expression resembling what we have today. There is, in fact, good evidence that the people responsible for adding the First Amendment to the Constitution would have been comfortable with forms of suppression that would be anathema today.

The central principles of the American system of freedom of expression, in other words, are not the product of a moment of inspired constitutional genius 200-plus years ago. We owe those principles, instead, to the living, common law Constitution. The central features of First Amendment law were hammered out in fits and starts, in a series of judicial decisions and extrajudicial developments, over the course of the twentieth century. The story of the emergence of the American constitutional law of free speech is a story of evolution and precedent, trial and error—a demonstration of how the living Constitution works.

THE CENTRAL PRINCIPLES OF THE FIRST AMENDMENT

The constitutional law governing freedom of expression is elaborate and complex. That very complexity gives the game away: obviously, one cannot simply read complicated principles off of the text of the First Amendment, and it is completely unrealistic to expect the people who adopted the First Amendment to have had a thorough understanding of all the contingencies to which the law would have to adapt. But the place to begin, as we look at how the living Constitution works in practice, is with three principles that are central to that body of law.

• The first principle is that it is important to protect the right to criticize the government. The Supreme Court, in the case of *New York Times v. Sullivan*, identified this as "the central meaning of the First Amendment": the government may not punish people for criticizing it or its officials. The three most important First Amendment cases of the last half-century have all concerned this principle.

New York Times v. Sullivan, decided in 1964, sharply limited the power of the government to force an individual to pay damages for defaming a public official. In *Brandenburg v. Ohio*, decided in 1969, the Supreme Court said that even "advocacy of the use of force" cannot be made illegal "except where such advocacy is directed to inciting or producing imminent lawless action and is likely to produce such action." And in *New York Times Co. v. United States*, decided in 1971, a majority of the Supreme Court ruled that the government would have to make a showing of extraordinary necessity (that a publication "will surely result in direct, immediate, and irreparable damage to our Nation or its people") before it could forbid newspapers to publish the Pentagon Papers—top secret documents that recounted the history of American involvement in the Vietnam War but that also, according to the government, revealed sensitive state and diplomatic secrets.

• The second principle is that not all speech should be protected as rigorously as speech criticizing the government. The Supreme Court has ruled that certain categories of low-value speech should receive less, or no, constitutional protection. Obscenity, commercial speech, false and defamatory statements, "fighting words," perjury, blackmail, threats, criminal solicitation—all of these are examples of low- or no-value speech. Speech in these categories can be restricted on the basis of a much weaker showing than is needed to protect high-value speech.

• The third principle is that there is a distinction among different kinds of regulations. Many laws affect people's ability to speak. A law that prohibits people from demonstrating in a way that blocks busy city streets during business hours presents different issues, and should be judged differently, from a law that restricts criticism of the president. Beyond that, many laws might, in practice, have a substantial but indirect effect on speech: for example, a Federal Reserve Board decision to raise interest rates—or any number of other government decisions—might ripple through the economy and drive many marginal publishing houses, bookstores, and periodicals out of business. But it would be unworkable to treat such decisions as presenting a serious First Amendment issue. Accordingly, the courts have elaborated distinctions among regulations that are based on the content of speech (for example, "No one may criticize the government"); regulations that are directed at speech but that are not based on the content of the speech (like the ban on rush-hour demonstrations); and "incidental" regulations that are directed at a wide range of activities (like the Federal Reserve example). Content-based regulations are ordinarily the most suspect; if they restrict high-value speech, they are presumed to be unconstitutional. Non-content-based regulations of speech may be carefully reviewed by the courts but are not assumed to be unconstitutional. Incidental restrictions are almost always constitutional, even if they have a substantial effect on speech.

These are just the basic contours of the American law of freedom of expression. But where do even these basic principles come from? Obviously, they are not explicit in the spare words of the First Amendment. In fact, they are in some ways difficult even to reconcile with the words of the First Amendment. They are also not to be found in the intentions or understandings of the framers of the First Amendment. To put the point bluntly but accurately, the text and the original understandings of the First Amendment are essentially irrelevant to the American system of freedom of expression as it exists today. The central principles of that system have been worked out by the courts, principally the Supreme Court, through a common law process: the living Constitution in action.

THE TEXT AND ITS PROBLEMS

The text of the First Amendment, which plays such a large role in popular understandings, actually presents significant problems. The first word of the amendment is "Congress." Taken at face value, the language of the amendment does not prohibit the president or the courts from restricting speech. No one today would suggest that the president or the courts may infringe free speech, but the principle that the First Amendment applies to the entire federal government, and not just to Congress, is difficult to square with the text of the Bill of Rights. The Second, Fourth, and Ninth Amendments refer to the rights of "the people"; the Fifth, Sixth, and Seventh Amendments speak in terms of the rights of individuals; the Third and Eighth Amendments forbid certain actions without limiting the prohibition to a certain branch of the government. The First Amendment could have been drafted with any of these locutions. But it wasn't; the First Amendment alone singles out Congress. If we focus just on the text, the case for protecting free speech against government infringement generally is actually somewhat weak.

Quite apart from that, it has been settled since the earliest days of the republic that the entire Bill of Rights, of its own force, applies only to the federal government, not to the states. So far as the First Amendment is concerned, then, for almost a hundred years the states were free to suppress speech in any way they wished. Today, the states are limited by the same First Amendment principles that apply to the federal government, but that is because the Fourteenth Amendment, added to the Constitution in 1868, has been interpreted to apply the First Amendment and most of the rest of the Bill of Rights to the states.

That interpretation, as I said in chapter 1, is also not obvious from the text or the original understandings. There is reason to believe that the drafters of the Fourteenth Amendment were, in fact, concerned about freedom of expression; antislavery speech was viciously suppressed in many slave states before the Civil War, and that experience was a recent and important memory for the members of the Reconstruction Congress. But the drafters of the Fourteenth Amendment did not include an explicit protection of free expression. The Fourteenth Amendment prohibits the states from denying anyone "liberty" without "due process of law" and from infringing the "privileges or immunities of citizens of the United States." Those are the clauses that are said to have "incorporated" the First Amendment. But on their face, those provisions do not protect speech from state regulation.

Beyond that, the text of the First Amendment simply does not tell us much. As Justice Black liked to say, "no law" means no law. But, as I noted in chapter 1, the relevant words that come after "no law" are "abridging the freedom of speech," and those words are not self-defining. It is not obvious what constitutes an abridgement, and it is not obvious what constitutes the freedom of speech. The complex set of First Amendment principles we have today is certainly one interpretation of that language. But many other principles—some protecting more speech, some protecting less—would also be perfectly consistent with the requirement that the government not "abridg[e]...the freedom of speech."

SEDITION AND "THOSE WHO WON OUR INDEPENDENCE"

Similarly, the evidence we have of the original understandings of the First Amendment does not support the idea that the framers meant to establish protections of free expression comparable to those with which we are familiar today. For much of the twentieth century, advocates of free speech invoked the framers for at least the central meaning of the First Amendment: the government may not punish political dissent. For example, Zechariah Chafee Jr., the first great First Amendment scholar of the twentieth century, asserted that the authors of the First Amendment intended to "make further prosecutions for criticism of the government, without any incitement to lawbreaking, forever impossible in the United States of America." Justice Oliver Wendell Holmes endorsed essentially this view in his famous dissenting opinion in the case of *Abrams v. United States*, decided in 1919, and Justice Louis Brandeis invoked "[t]hose who won our independence" in his brilliant concurring opinion in *Whitney v. California*, decided in 1927.

You might think that, even if the framers and ratifiers of the First Amendment could not have anticipated all the twists and turns the law would take, they at least gave us this basic principle: the First Amendment is primarily there to guarantee a right to criticize the government. But even on this central issue, it is, notwithstanding Chafee and Holmes and Brandeis, simply not clear what the original understandings were. To some extent, the issue is just the problem, endemic to originalism, of trying to understand the world of late eighteenth-century America: how people then saw their world and what they hoped to accomplish by adopting various legal provisions. But to the extent that we *can* reconstruct the original understandings, we do not find unequivocal support for what we now call "the

central meaning of the First Amendment." A few points, in particular, stand out.

• When the framers adopted the First Amendment, they were
concerned with the balance of power between the federal
government and the states and not just about protecting free
expression in general. The entire focus of the debate over the First
Amendment was on the federal government and on making clear
that the Constitution's grants of various powers to Congress did not
include the power to restrict speech or the press. The idea that the
First Amendment would establish a nationwide principle that
speech must be free from the control of government, period, was
not part of the original understanding.

• Even as far as the federal government was concerned, it
is—remarkably—not at all clear that the original understanding was
that the First Amendment would prevent the government from
punishing its critics. There was a robust tradition in England of
punishing political dissent—"seditious libel," it was called. As Chief
Justice John Holt explained in 1704: "If people should not be called
to account for possessing the people with an ill opinion of the
government, no government can subsist. For it is very necessary for
all governments that the people should have a good opinion of it."
Even truthful statements about the government were therefore
subject to criminal penalties; in fact, truthful statements were
especially threatening to the stability of the government, and
therefore especially worthy of punishment.

William Blackstone—"whose works," according to the Supreme
Court, "constituted the preeminent authority on English law for the
founding generation"—defined freedom of expression to include
only freedom from "previous restraints upon publication," such as
laws requiring that a newspaper publisher receive permission from a

censor before publication. For Blackstone, freedom of speech and the press simply did not have anything to do with after-the-fact criminal punishment for speech. In fact, Blackstone vigorously endorsed suppression of a kind we would consider unthinkable today: "to punish (as the law does at present) any dangerous or offensive writings, which, when published, shall on a fair and impartial trial be adjudged of a pernicious tendency, is necessary for the preservation of peace and good order, of government and religion, the only foundations of civil liberty."

Some historians argue that the First Amendment was understood to repudiate Blackstone and to abolish the crime of seditious libel, but that is far from clear. In part, this is a textbook illustration of some of the problems with originalism: the differences between the framers' world and ours, and the difficulty of translating their views into our world. For example, the framers of the First Amendment had much more confidence in the ability and willingness of juries to protect dissident speech than we have today. The framers seem to have thought that protecting the right to a trial by jury and narrowing the definition of treason (both of which were accomplished by the original Constitution and the Bill of Rights) would provide enough protection for political dissent. That belief might have been correct in the eighteenth century, but by our standards today those measures alone are inadequate. One lesson we have drawn from 200 years of experience is that juries, which reflect the views widely held in society, can't be counted on to protect unpopular dissenters, especially at times when people feel endangered by foreign governments or internal upheaval. What do we make of the original understandings when circumstances have changed in such a way? Originalism doesn't give us an answer.

• To the extent that we can determine the original understandings, there is a good argument that the First Amendment was *not* understood to outlaw prosecutions for seditious libel. There were some prosecutions for seditious libel in states that had adopted provisions like the First Amendment in their own state constitutions—suggesting that the original understanding of the language of the First Amendment permitted such prosecutions. And in 1798, Congress—with the affirmative votes of many of the framers of the First Amendment—enacted the Sedition Act, a federal law that expressly punished dissent. The Sedition Act controversy was highly partisan, and many of the various claims made at the time about the meaning of the First Amendment were offered for partisan purposes and so cannot be accepted at face value. Some framers, including James Madison, the most important figure in the drafting of the Bill of Rights, condemned the Sedition Act as a violation of the First Amendment. But other framers, including John Adams and Alexander Hamilton, defended the act. So there are serious doubts about whether the founding generation understood the First Amendment to stand even for what is, for us today, the central principle of a system of free expression.

• Finally, once we move beyond the core area of dissent and criticism of the government, there is little doubt that the framers accepted many forms of suppression that we today would consider incompatible with the First Amendment. For example, there were prosecutions for blasphemy even in states that had First Amendment–like constitutional provisions. Defamation was considered outside the protection of any principle of free expression. Today, a prosecution for blasphemy would be unthinkable, and defamation law is subject to many important constitutional restrictions, even in cases that do not involve public officials.

FREEDOM OF EXPRESSION AND THE COMMON
LAW APPROACH

The American system of freedom of expression, as we know it, did not begin to emerge as a coherent body of legal principles until well into the twentieth century—in opinions written in a series of cases decided just after the First World War. Those principles emerged in a way that was, in most respects, typical of the common law.

Three characteristics of this process stand out. First, the process was evolutionary; the key principles were developed over fifty years, often through trial and error, with many false starts and subsequent corrections. Second, throughout the process, the Supreme Court relied most heavily on earlier judicial decisions. There was no serious parsing of the text of the Constitution, and in no case was the text or the original understandings decisive. In fact—and this may tell us all we need to know about originalism—the relationship between the law and the original understandings was essentially backward: as the principles governing freedom of expression were hammered out, those principles were attributed to the original understandings, without serious attention to the historical record.

Third, the development of the principles was marked by an unmistakable concern with matters of policy and political morality— a concern with what kinds of First Amendment principles would make sense and achieve good results. This explicit consideration of matters of policy, fairness, workability, and political morality— within relatively narrow limits—is, of course, a characteristic of the common law method. The principles that we today think of as "the First Amendment" don't come from the text or the original under- standings; they are instead, in Burke's words, an "edifice" that is accepted because it "has answered in [a] tolerable degree for...the common purposes of society."

CLEAR AND PRESENT DANGER

The evolutionary process that led to today's First Amendment began uncertainly, to say the least. In 1919, in *Schenck v. United States*, Justice Holmes—who is ultimately one of the heroes of the story—wrote an opinion for the Court upholding the suppression of speech. Schenck had, during World War I, circulated a leaflet condemning conscription, in "impassioned language," as immoral and unconstitutional. Schenck circulated the leaflet to men who had been called for military service and was convicted of violating a federal law prohibiting obstruction of the draft. Holmes emphasized that the speech occurred during wartime and that a jury could have found that its "tendency" and "intent" were to obstruct the draft.

The most significant contribution of the *Schenck* opinion turned out to be Holmes's statement that "[t]he question in every case is whether the words used are used in such circumstances and are of such a nature as to create a clear and present danger that they will bring about the substantive evils that Congress has a right to prevent." The so-called clear-and-present-danger test, here used by Holmes to uphold the suppression of speech, became integral to the development of the law—and even to the common cultural understanding—of freedom of expression. The phrase "clear and present danger" may be as well known as the words of the First Amendment itself. Many people, no doubt, think those words are in the text of the U.S. Constitution. And in some sense, they might as well be: those words have been far more important in the development of the law than have the actual words of the First Amendment. "Clear and present danger," a phrase that occurs in a judicial opinion but not in the text of the Constitution or in the original understandings, took root because, over time, that phrase proved to capture something important and valuable about the protection of free speech. That is the way the living Constitution works.

After *Schenck*, the next critical step came several months later, in *Abrams v. United States.* The Supreme Court in *Abrams* upheld another World War I conviction, but this time Holmes, along with Brandeis, dissented and sided with the speaker. Holmes's opinion asserted that the clear-and-present-danger test required the government to show a high-probability risk of harm that is both immediate and serious: "we should be eternally vigilant against attempts to check the expression of opinions that we loathe... unless they so imminently threaten immediate interference with the lawful and pressing purposes of the law that an immediate check is required to save the country."

This understanding of clear and present danger—with many variations and refinements over time—has become a core principle of First Amendment law. It is not enough that speech might cause harm. It is not even enough that speech is likely to cause harm. The harm has to be imminent, and serious. Versions of this test appear in the Pentagon Papers case and in *Brandenburg.* If there was a single, inspired moment at which the central feature of the American system of freedom of expression was decreed, it was not the adoption of the First Amendment; it was Holmes's dissent in *Abrams*.

But there was no such moment. Holmes's opinion was a dissent. It made no law. The principle of Holmes's *Abrams* opinion became law, but only because later opinions gradually adopted Holmes's approach over the course of the next half-century. That approach had broad cultural resonance and, ultimately, it seemed to work well. In these ways, the development of free speech in the United States followed the model of common law evolution that is the defining feature of our living Constitution.

In the first phase of this evolution, Holmes and Brandeis continued to urge their version of the First Amendment—using the clear-

and-present-danger test as it was understood in *Abrams*—even though a majority of the Supreme Court repeatedly disagreed with them and upheld the suppression of speech. All of the decisions in this period, between 1919 and 1927, involved political speech that was highly critical of the government—either speech critical of the war, or speech advocating some form of radical change, generally anarchist or socialist. The Court allowed the speakers to be punished on the theory that it was rational for the government to conclude that this speech could cause harm. Schenck's speech, for example, might not only have persuaded people to change their minds about the wisdom of the war; it might also have caused draftees to refuse induction.

Holmes and Brandeis understood that this approach allowed dissident speech to be suppressed too easily. Speech that is critical of government policies will often have some tendency to cause harm. Almost any criticism of the government might, for example, encourage people to violate the laws that the speaker criticizes. When the speaker's views are unpopular, it will be too easy for the government—quite possibly reflecting the dominant sentiment of the population—to seize on that potentially harmful tendency as an excuse for suppressing speech that it actually dislikes because the speech is critical of government policies. As a result, the approach taken by the Court in this period could easily have led to a climate in which it would be impossible to criticize the government without risking punishment. Holmes and Brandeis, in opposing this view of the First Amendment, embraced what *New York Times v. Sullivan* later called "the central meaning of the First Amendment." Their dissents provided the raw material from which later justices fashioned First Amendment doctrine protecting political dissent. But this battle was won slowly, over time, as it gradually became clear that political speech should have the kind of protection that Holmes's *Abrams* dissent envisioned.

THE EMERGENCE OF PROTECTION

The Court did not actually uphold a free speech claim until 1931, when it reversed the conviction of a woman who had violated a state law forbidding her to display a red flag "as a sign, symbol, or emblem of opposition to organized government." The opinion in that case, *Stromberg v. California,* rested mostly on technical grounds—that the law was too vague—but it did treat as axiomatic the proposition that the government could not punish people for urging changes in the law or the government by lawful means.

Stromberg was representative of a series of cases involving dissident speech that the Court decided in the 1930s. The Court upheld the claims of the speakers, but it did so usually on relatively technical grounds that did not purport to alter the rulings from which Holmes and Brandeis had dissented and that did not establish any broad, new First Amendment principles. But aspects of the Holmes-Brandeis position were working their way into the law incrementally, as in *Stromberg.*

Another important development was the Court's 1939 decision in *Schneider v. State,* which held unconstitutional a municipal ordinance that forbade the distribution of leaflets on public streets. This was the first time that the Court had squarely addressed a non-content-based restriction on speech, and one can find in the opinion in *Schneider* the basis of almost all of the current law in this area. The Court implicitly recognized that such a restriction presented different issues from a restriction on the content of speech. At the same time, the Court carefully reviewed the ordinance; it did not simply defer to the municipality's judgment. With some refinements, that is how the Court treats non-content-based restrictions today.

Just fourteen years before *Schneider,* in *Gitlow v. New York*—one of the decisions from which Holmes and Brandeis dissented—the

Supreme Court had upheld a state law that directly forbade the advocacy of "the duty, necessity, or propriety of overthrowing...the government by force or violence." The opinion in *Gitlow* had emphasized the importance of deferring to legislative judgments about the dangerousness of speech. The ordinance in *Schneider* was much less threatening to the core purposes of free expression than the law in *Gitlow*. Yet the Court in *Schneider* had little difficulty in second-guessing the legislative judgment that underlay that ordinance.

This was a remarkable change in the Court's approach. A healthy system of freedom of expression probably could survive if *Schneider* had come out the other way—if legislatures generally could enact whatever non-content-based restrictions they wanted. *Gitlow*, by contrast, deferred to the legislature in a context in which popular opinion is likely to be inflamed against a speaker and in which suppression might badly distort public deliberation. What accounted for the change in the Court's view? The Constitution, obviously, had not been formally amended.

The answer must lie in the evolutionary workings of the living Constitution, both in and out of the courts. Beginning with the Russian Revolution and World War I and continuing into the 1920s, popular and government reaction to dissidents was overwrought and panic-stricken; by the 1930s, that panic had abated. *Schneider*, decided in 1939, came after a series of victories—in *Stromberg* and other cases—by parties claiming rights under the First Amendment. So, by the end of the 1930s, the free speech edifice (to use Burke's term) no longer consisted of just the post–World War I decisions; there were now a number of cases upholding speakers' claims, and there was a trend, however incompletely rationalized, toward protecting speech. The Court accordingly had a solid common law basis for saying that laws restricting speech should be more closely scrutinized. Again, it was the ebb and flow of precedent, not the text of the Constitution or the original understandings, that accounted for the shape of the law.

In the early 1940s, the Court picked up these pieces—the Holmes-Brandeis dissents, the trend toward protecting speech, and the view, no doubt prompted in part by events in Europe, that the protection of civil liberties was vitally important—and molded them into highly speech-protective principles that foreshadowed today's. In *Thornhill v. Alabama*, decided in 1940, the Court upheld the right to engage in labor picketing and stated, as if it had been law all along, a version of the clear-and-present-danger test that echoed Holmes's *Abrams* dissent: "Abridgement of the liberty of... discussion can be justified only where the clear danger of substantive evils arises under circumstances affording no opportunity to test the merits of ideas by competition for acceptance in the market of public opinion." *Cantwell v. Connecticut*, decided later in 1940, suggested that the clear-and-present-danger test, in its Holmes-Brandeis version, was the appropriate standard for a case in which a speaker was prosecuted because his speech antagonized his audience— an important, but distinct, principle in a system of freedom of expression. In 1941, in *Bridges v. California*, the Court used the same test to overturn a conviction for contempt of court, where the speaker's criticisms of a state court allegedly interfered with the administration of justice. By 1943, in *West Virginia State Board of Education v. Barnette*, the Court could announce: "It is now a commonplace that censorship or suppression of expression of opinion is tolerated by our Constitution only when the expression presents a clear and present danger" of unlawful action. These four opinions were written by four different justices, and they involved markedly different situations. The First Amendment had become, in significant part, the Holmes-Brandeis version of the clear-and-present-danger test. A substantial part of the present-day edifice was in place. But it emerged not through any single decisive act of constitution-making, and certainly not because of some new discoveries about the original understanding of the First Amendment. It emerged through the case-by-case process that is characteristic of the common law.

One other decision in the 1940s is noteworthy for the effect it had in shaping the law. In *Chaplinsky v. New Hampshire*, decided in 1942, the Court upheld the conviction of an individual for using "fighting words," which it defined as words "which by their very utterance inflict injury or tend to incite an immediate breach of the peace." In the course of its opinion, the Court asserted that "[t]here are certain well-defined and narrowly limited classes of speech, the prevention and punishment of which have never been thought to raise any Constitutional problem. These include the lewd and obscene, the profane, the libelous, and the insulting or 'fighting' words." This was the Court's first clear statement of the distinction between low-value and high-value speech, as well as a clear statement of the important corollary that speech is of high value unless it falls into one of the low-value categories.

This distinction has structured modern First Amendment doctrine, even though at first glance it might seem questionable. The text of the First Amendment does not suggest a difference between high-value and low-value speech, and the idea that courts are to assess the "value" of speech seems problematic. But the distinction between high- and low-value speech was again an outgrowth of the evolution of First Amendment doctrine. Once the Court had begun to place political speech at the center of the system of freedom of expression, and to afford extraordinary protection to political speech, it was forced to recognize that not all speech could be treated the same way. No one believes that a fraudulent "phishing" e-mail deserves the same extraordinary protection as political dissent, and if the Court were to treat all speech alike, it would end up watering down the protection of the speech that it is most important to protect. Given the evolution of First Amendment law, the Court came to understand that it would have to make some kind of distinction between speech that was entitled to the greatest protection and speech that was not.

The distinction did not, of course, have to be drawn in just the way *Chaplinsky* drew it. *Chaplinsky* differentiated between categories of speech; the Court could have said that it would proceed in each case to assess the value of the particular speech involved. And the Court could have established high-value categories and made low-value speech the default position. For a time, it was unclear whether the categorical approach of *Chaplinsky* would prevail. But the Court worked these matters out, in common law fashion, beginning in the 1950s.

THE MCCARTHY ERA
AND THE *BRANDENBURG* SYNTHESIS

In the 1950s, free speech issues became more contentious, politically, than they had been at any time since World War I. Most of the cases involved laws directed at people suspected of being, or of having been, members of the Communist Party. The most important case was *Dennis v. United States*, decided in 1951, which upheld the convictions of leaders of the Communist Party of the United States for conspiring to advocate the overthrow of the U.S. government by force or violence. A plurality of the Supreme Court (there was no majority opinion) upheld the convictions on the basis of a version of the clear-and-present-danger test that said the critical question was "whether the gravity of the 'evil,' discounted by its improbability, justifies such invasion of free speech as is necessary to avoid the danger."

This version of the test—essentially, a kind of cost-benefit balancing—was sharply different from the Holmes-Brandeis test, descended from *Abrams*, which required that the harm be both imminent and highly probable. The *Dennis* test instead asked judges to decide whether the expected costs of the harm "justifie[d]" the restriction on speech. This approach lent itself quite readily to the kind of deference to the legislature that was endorsed in *Gitlow* and effectively repudiated in *Schneider* and other cases, and indeed Justice Felix Frankfurter wrote a concurring opinion that called explicitly for deference to the legislature—the deferential position that has now had no adherents on the Supreme Court for decades.

In the years after *Dennis*, the clear-and-present-danger test, so dominant in the early 1940s, came under attack from many sides. One set of critics considered *Dennis* to be an abomination, and they thought the clear-and-present-danger test was at fault. *Dennis* had permitted dissidents to be punished simply for advocacy. Justices Hugo Black and William Douglas, among others, came to the view that the clear-and-present-danger test had proved itself too flexible to stand up to anti-Communist hysteria. Other critics said that the problem with the clear-and-present-danger test was that it simplified complex issues. They reacted against the use of the test in areas outside its original context of dissident political speech. The clear-and-present-danger test was not well suited to determining, for example, when labor picketing should be regulated. Many of these critics thought that the only plausible way to interpret the clear-and-present-danger test was as calling for a kind of cost-benefit balancing, as in *Dennis*.

In terms of the common law approach, the clear-and-present-danger test, so attractive at one point, had overreached its proper scope and, in *Dennis*, had—according to some—failed Cardozo's test of the "final cause" of the law: the clear-and-present-danger approach had proved incapable of accomplishing its most important objectives. Following *Dennis*, the clear-and-present-danger test went into eclipse. The Court itself backed away from both *Dennis* and clear and present danger later in the 1950s. In *Yates v. United States*, for example, decided in 1957, the Court held that the Smith Act, the statute under which both the *Dennis* and the *Yates* defendants were charged, did not prohibit "advocacy of abstract doctrine" even if that advocacy were "engaged in with the intent to accomplish overthrow" of the government. Rather, the Court held, the Smith Act prohibited only "advocacy directed at promoting unlawful action."

This distinction—between advocacy of ideas and advocacy of action—was, like clear and present danger, derived not from the text or the original understandings of the First Amendment but from the resources that the living Constitution made available to the Court: the distinction between high- and low-value speech. The best way to understand the distinction drawn in *Yates* is that advocacy of ideas is high-value speech, while expressly urging people to violate the law is low-value.

The most recent step in this evolution is *Brandenburg v. Ohio*. There, the Court said that the First Amendment protects even the express advocacy of force or lawbreaking "except where such advocacy is directed to inciting or producing imminent lawless action and is likely to produce such action." *Brandenburg* was the product of two strands of well-developed twentieth-century legal evolution. *Brandenburg* does not use the phrase "clear and present danger," but the Court's emphasis on imminence and likelihood of harm was derived directly from the Holmes and Brandeis version of the clear-and-present-danger test. *Brandenburg* appears to have added to that test a requirement that the speech be of low value; if the government wants to restrict speech, it must show that the speech is not the advocacy of ideas but is rather "directed to inciting or producing imminent lawless action."

In *Brandenburg*, the Court concluded that, although the Holmes-Brandeis test captured something important about the First Amendment, that test was not sufficient by itself. The evidence for that conclusion was the product of trial and error: specifically, the use to which the test had been put in *Dennis*. In the crucible of common law testing, clear and present danger collapsed too easily into a simple balancing of costs and benefits. So in *Brandenburg*, the Court combined the Holmes-Brandeis line of precedents with *Chaplinsky* and *Yates*—cases that emphasized the distinction between high- and low-value speech. The building blocks of the *Brandenburg* synthesis were thus entirely the product of precedents—precedents that were tested and modified by being applied in case after case, just as the common law approach suggests.

NEW YORK TIMES V. SULLIVAN
AND THE PENTAGON PAPERS CASE

The other mainstays of current First Amendment law also represent the final (so far) stage in the evolution of the living Constitution on the common law model. *New York Times v. Sullivan* held that a public official cannot recover damages for defamation without proving not just that the defamatory statement was false, but that the defendant made the statement with knowledge that it was false or with reckless disregard of the risk of falsehood. *Sullivan* is another decision that originalists would have to reject; even the most deter-mined originalists have to concede that the First Amendment, when it was adopted, was not understood to interfere with traditional private libel or slander actions for damages.

Justice William Brennan's opinion for the Court in *Sullivan* did not suggest that the decision was supported by the original understandings. On the contrary: Justice Brennan referred to "the great controversy over the Sedition Act of 1798, which first crystallized a national awareness of the central meaning of the First Amendment." The Sedition Act—which had been supported by many framers of the Constitution—was, Justice Brennan said, repudiated by "the court of history."

New York Times v. Sullivan did not come out of nowhere. The speech in *Sullivan*—which criticized public officials for violating the rights of civil rights demonstrators in the South—was political speech. By the time *Sullivan* was decided, the Holmes and Brandeis approach—and its acceptance by subsequent cases—strongly supported *Sullivan*'s explicit conclusion that this kind of speech is at the center of the First Amendment. *Sullivan* broke new ground because it held that the law of defamation—one of the oldest branches of tort law, which historically was entirely the province of the states—was to be strictly limited by the First Amendment. But in achieving this breakthrough, *Sullivan* again had specific support in the precedents. A case decided as early as 1931, *Near v. Minnesota*, had protected speech that defamed a public official. *Bridges*, on which the Court in *Sullivan* relied, held—on the basis of the Holmes-Brandeis test—that the First Amendment protected severe criticism of a judge. *Sullivan* was an important further step in the direction of emphasizing the protection of political dissent, but it was far from the first step. Thus *Sullivan*, too, fits in the common law model—certainly far better than it accords with the original intentions of the framers. And once *Sullivan* was decided, it led to a series of further decisions, in common law fashion, that have effectively constitutionalized the law of defamation.

In the Pentagon Papers case, *New York Times Co. v. United States,* the Supreme Court ruled that the First Amendment barred the government from preventing the publication, in the *New York Times* and the *Washington Post,* of classified government documents that described internal deliberations and other information about the Vietnam War. Most of the justices in the majority emphasized that the government was trying to impose a prior restraint on the publication of the papers, and they asserted, echoing Blackstone, that prior restraints are anathema to a system of freedom of expression. To that extent, the Pentagon Papers decision can be traced to the intentions of the framers.

But the concern with prior restraint cannot, by itself, explain the Pentagon Papers case. The Pentagon Papers revealed material that was of central importance to citizens seeking to understand the most controversial political issue of the time, and that fact unquestionably played a role in the Court's decision. For one thing, while the opinions in the Pentagon Papers case emphasized that the First Amendment forbids prior restraint, it is difficult to believe that the Court would have allowed the newspaper editors to be punished for a crime after they published the papers. In addition, the standard that the Court appears to have established—that publication may not be restrained unless it "will surely result in direct, immediate, and irreparable damage to our Nation or its people"—is an even stronger version of the Holmes-Brandeis clear-and-present-danger test. So the Pentagon Papers decision, too, is a direct product of the central theme in the evolution of the law of the First Amendment in the twentieth century: the vital importance of protecting speech on political matters, particularly speech that vigorously questions government policies, even if that speech might also have some harmful consequences. That central theme emerged from the evolutionary process that is characteristic of our living Constitution.

The American law of freedom of expression—a constitutional success story—did not emerge from the text of the U.S. Constitution or from the original understandings. But it was also not simply created by a few judges who, luckily for us, happened to get things right. That body of law has been, instead, the product of common law evolution. It developed over time, fitfully, by a process in which principles and standards were tried and sometimes eventually accepted, sometimes abandoned, sometimes modified, in light of experience and an ongoing, explicit assessment of whether they were sound as a matter of policy. The law of the First Amendment is a creation of the living Constitution.

CHAPTER FOUR

Brown v. Board of Education and Innovation in the Living Constitution

(with a Note on Roe v. Wade)

BROWN V. BOARD OF EDUCATION, the 1954 decision that outlawed racial segregation in public schools, is also a remarkable constitutional success story. Some of the important First Amendment decisions were controversial, but *Brown* was more than controversial. It was reviled by defenders of segregation. Many southern members of Congress signed the "Southern Manifesto," which denounced *Brown* as illegitimate and asserted that states had the right to defy it. School districts in many parts of the South vowed "massive resistance" to the decision.

More interesting, even some people who despised segregation thought that *Brown* was a lawless decision. We know from private papers that several justices who were part of the unanimous Court in *Brown* were initially unsure what to do because, while they opposed segregation, they were troubled about whether the Court could lawfully declare segregation to be unconstitutional. Herbert Wechsler, a law professor who helped the civil rights lawyers prepare their case in *Brown*, later wrote that *Brown* could not be justified in principled legal terms.

Today, *Brown* is not just accepted; it is an icon. The lawfulness of *Brown* is a fixed point for the mainstream legal culture. Anyone who doubts that *Brown* is lawful is a fringe player, at best. It is, for example, inconceivable that anyone could get appointed, or confirmed, to a federal judgeship if it became known that he or she thought that *Brown* was unlawful. There is disagreement about the practical effects of *Brown*: little school desegregation actually happened for a decade after *Brown* was decided, until the Civil Rights Act of 1964 gave the executive branch the power to cut off federal funds to school districts that refused to desegregate. But *Brown*'s status as a decision of unquestioned validity—indeed, in the eyes of many, as the Supreme Court's finest hour—is central to understanding American constitutional law.

So any theory about the U.S. Constitution must explain, and justify, *Brown*. Originalism, notoriously, comes up short. As I said earlier, *Brown* is not simply unsupported by the original understandings; it is not just that the original understandings are unclear on the question whether school segregation is permissible, in the way that they are perhaps unclear about seditious libel. *Brown* seems to be flatly inconsistent with the original understandings. The original understanding of the Fourteenth Amendment seems to have been quite clearly that school segregation was allowed, that the amendment permitted racial segregation in public schools to continue. While there have been some notable revisionist efforts to claim otherwise, that is still the consensus view.

Understandably, given *Brown*'s status, originalists do not conclude that *Brown* was just wrong. Instead, with rare (and, again, fringe) exceptions, originalists struggle to come up with explanations of how *Brown* is consistent with the original understandings, once those understandings are properly characterized. The usual maneuver is of the kind I mentioned earlier: changing the level of generality by asserting that the Fourteenth Amendment, properly viewed, enshrined a principle of racial equality. As I have said, once that kind of maneuver is allowed, originalists can justify anything, and the principal claim of originalists—that their approach, unlike living constitutionalism, really limits judges—becomes obviously false.

The concern about the lawfulness of *Brown* was not just a product of originalism, however. When *Brown* was decided, originalism was not much in vogue. A big part of the worry about *Brown* was that it had to overrule (in fact, even if not technically) a Supreme Court precedent. The precedent was *Plessy v. Ferguson*, an 1896 decision that had upheld a Louisiana law requiring railroads to provide "equal but separate accommodations for the white and colored races." The theory behind *Plessy* was that the Fourteenth Amendment required only equality, and segregated facilities could still be equal. That notion—that segregation is compatible with equality—was also, apparently, accepted at the time of the Fourteenth Amendment. The concern about *Brown* was whether there was any legal basis to overturn the principle of "separate but equal," sanctified as it was by *Plessy* as well as the original understandings.

Perhaps *Brown* should just be viewed as a lawless but morally necessary decision. On this understanding, *Brown* was a kind of mini coup d'état. But I think we can do better than that. *Brown* didn't come out of the text and the original understandings, but it also didn't come out of nowhere.

The common law, as I have mentioned, does not treat precedents as untouchable; sometimes, precedents can be overruled. Exactly when they can be overruled is a complex matter, but there is at least one well-established pattern of overruling in the common law. And *Brown* conforms, to a remarkable degree, to that pattern. Once we understand that our Constitution is not just the text, and not just the original understandings—but is a living constitution that evolves as the common law does—*Brown* begins to look, if not routine, unquestionably lawful.

COMMON LAW INNOVATION IN ACTION: *MACPHERSON V. BUICK MOTOR CO.*

In order to see how *Brown* follows a traditional common law pattern, it's useful, first, to see the common law in its native habitat, so to speak, in one of the most famous examples of common law innovation: Judge Benjamin Cardozo's opinion in a case called *MacPherson v. Buick Motor Co.*, decided in 1916. Cardozo, who later joined the Supreme Court, was probably the most celebrated American common law judge of the twentieth century. *MacPherson* was one of his most famous opinions, and it has become a classic in the common law canon: it certainly has its critics, but more often it has been held out as reflecting common law reasoning in its most sophisticated form.

MacPherson was what we would now call a product liability case, but it arose at a time when it was not entirely clear that consumers could sue manufacturers for injuries caused by defective products. Buick Motor Company negligently made a car with a defective wheel, and Mrs. MacPherson was ultimately injured because of the defect. The question was whether she could recover damages for her injury.

What made *MacPherson* a difficult case at the time was that there were no direct dealings—there was no contract—between Buick, the manufacturer, and MacPherson, the consumer. Buick sold the car to a retailer, and it was the retailer who dealt with the MacPhersons.

At the time, the generally accepted common law rule in such cases was the so-called privity-of-contract requirement. Manufacturers were not liable to any party with whom they did not have a contract, even if the product they made was defective, and even if the defect was the result of the manufacturer's carelessness. Usually, that meant that manufacturers were not liable to the ultimate consumer, because most products are sold through wholesalers and retailers.

The privity-of-contract rule apparently originated in the English case of *Winterbottom v. Wright*, decided in 1842. Privity of contract was explicitly adopted in New York state in 1852, in *Thomas v. Winchester*. At the same time, though, New York and other states recognized an exception for "inherently dangerous" objects. A consumer could recover from a manufacturer for injuries caused by an inherently dangerous object, even if there was no privity of contract. *Thomas v. Winchester* itself involved such an object—a mislabeled bottle of "medicine" that actually contained poison—and so, notwithstanding the privity rule, the plaintiff in *Thomas* prevailed.

For the next sixty years, New York courts decided cases under this regime, in which the privity requirement barred a product liability action unless the product in question was inherently dangerous. The issue in each case was whether a particular defective product was inherently dangerous or not. In 1870, the New York Court of Appeals ruled that a flywheel in a machine was not an inherently dangerous object. The court explained: "Poison is a dangerous subject. Gunpowder is the same. A torpedo is a dangerous instrument, as is a spring gun, a loaded rifle, or the like." But a flywheel, like "an ordinary carriage wheel, a wagon axle, or the common chair in which we sit" was not inherently dangerous, so the privity requirement applied and the injured plaintiff could not recover from the manufacturer. A few years later, the court held that a steam boiler was also not an inherently dangerous object.

Over the next three decades, though, the New York courts decided that scaffolding, a defective building, an elevator, and a rope supplied to lift heavy goods all fell within the exception for inherently dangerous objects. In 1908, the New York Court of Appeals ruled that a bottle of "aerated water" was inherently dangerous. In 1909, that same court held that a large coffee urn was inherently dangerous.

In all of these New York cases, the courts said they were just applying the accepted rule: a plaintiff had to show privity of contract unless a product was inherently dangerous. None of the later cases, in which plaintiffs repeatedly won, questioned the authority of the earlier cases. The later cases just kept ruling, one after another, that the product fell within the "inherently dangerous" exception of the well-established rule.

That was the state of the law when *MacPherson* came before Cardozo's court. *MacPherson*, as I said, involved an automobile with a defective wheel, and there was no privity of contract between the plaintiff and the manufacturer of the automobile. The lawyers in the case, not surprisingly, agreed that the issue was whether an automobile was an inherently dangerous product. Mrs. MacPherson's lawyer said that a car was an inherently dangerous object, so Mrs. MacPherson's claim fell within the exception to the privity rule. Buick's lawyer said that a car did not fall within the exception, so the privity rule applied and protected Buick from liability.

Cardozo's opinion dispatched the privity requirement altogether. Instead of requiring privity, with an exception for inherently dangerous products, the court held that a negligent manufacturer would be liable to anyone who could foreseeably be hurt by its negligence. Many other states soon followed *MacPherson* and repudiated the privity rule, allowing consumers to recover from manufacturers whenever they could demonstrate negligence and foreseeability.

The exact meaning of those requirements isn't important; the law in this area has moved on since Cardozo's time. What is important is the justification for Cardozo's decision to refuse to do what so many earlier judges had done—decide whether the product was or wasn't within the inherently dangerous exception—and instead simply to scrap the privity requirement entirely.

While Cardozo was circumspect, he left little doubt that he thought the privity requirement was a bad idea as a matter of policy. He did not claim that his decision was squarely dictated by the legal materials alone, and in his extrajudicial writings (such as the passage I quoted in chapter 2), he explicitly asserted that judges sometimes had to consider what made sense as a matter of policy. But what makes *MacPherson* an exemplar of common law reasoning is that Cardozo did not stop with his policy views but instead drew on the lessons provided by the earlier cases—two lessons in particular.

First, the earlier cases had demonstrated that the privity regime was no longer workable. At one time, perhaps, it was possible to distinguish between inherently dangerous objects and objects that were (in the words of another old English case) part of "the ordinary intercourse of life." But by the time of *MacPherson*, that distinction had broken down. Too many things were *both* inherently dangerous *and* part of the ordinary intercourse of life. Courts applying the distinction had decided that a steam boiler was not inherently dangerous but a coffee urn and a bottle of aerated water were. *MacPherson* then presented the question of how to classify an automobile. The question was unanswerable; the governing rule had broken down. A regime in which a steam boiler is classified as less dangerous than a bottle of aerated water is beyond repair. Cardozo's conclusion that the privity rule had to be discarded was supported not just by his own views about good policy but by several decades' experience that had demonstrated that the rule was unworkable.

The second lesson of the earlier cases was that, while the courts were purporting to apply the privity regime—and no doubt generally believed that they were, to the best of their ability, applying the privity regime—they were, quite possibly without knowing it, gravitating to a new rule. Cardozo was able to claim, plausibly for the most part, that whatever the opinions said in the earlier cases, the *outcomes* of those cases were consistent with the principle that a manufacturer is liable for foreseeable injuries caused by its negligence. That was true even though the reasoning of the earlier cases was based on the privity regime and the inherently dangerous exception. It was particularly true of the more recent cases—the scaffolding, coffee urn, and aerated water cases—which made much more sense if they were understood as applications of the foreseeability rule rather than the "inherently dangerous" exception that they purported to apply.

Cardozo was, therefore, in a position to argue that his ultimate conclusion—that the privity regime should be discarded in favor of a simple requirement of foreseeability—not only was good policy but was implicitly supported by several decades' worth of decisions. Even though those decisions professed adherence to the privity rule with its inherently dangerous exception, they actually demonstrated both that the privity regime was not workable and that courts, perhaps without being fully aware of what they were doing, were moving to a simple foreseeability requirement. The combination of normative reasoning and a reliance on the lessons of the past—with a recognition that both are indispensable—is what makes *MacPherson* a common law exemplar. The conclusion that the privity regime was unworkable and should be replaced by foreseeability was, in a sense, not just Cardozo's alone. It was a conclusion that the earlier judges had also gradually reached, over several decades, even though those judges did not acknowledge the evolution in the law. Cardozo's innovation consisted of making that conclusion, reached inexplicitly in fits and starts, fully explicit.

BROWN AND COMMON LAW OVERRULING

Once we recognize that we have a living constitution, in the sense described by the common law method, we no longer have to regard *Brown* as inexplicable or as a lawless act that just turned out well. That is because *Brown* can be justified as a decision that was reached on the basis of the common law method. The cases leading up to *Brown*—in a development that resembles the line of cases preceding *MacPherson*—had already left "separate but equal" in a shambles. *Brown* was the completion of an evolutionary, common law process, not an isolated, pathbreaking act.

Plessy, decided in 1896, had upheld a state law requiring separate-but-equal accommodations on railroads. But rigid racial segregation had shallower roots in the South than many once supposed; so-called Jim Crow laws requiring segregation were not instituted systematically after the abolition of slavery but rather became widespread in the South only in the late nineteenth century. This was the argument of C. Vann Woodward's *The Strange Career of Jim Crow*, published in 1957 but based on research that was available to the Court earlier, and the opinion in *Brown* made a point of noting that "'separate but equal' did not make its appearance in this court until 1896." That itself is relevant, under the common law approach. Separate but equal was not as well established a tradition as the segregationists claimed, and the Burkean case for it was correspondingly weaker.

In the two decades following *Plessy*, the Court applied the separate-but-equal principle in two cases involving education without reconsidering whether that principle was sound. But at the same time, the Court sowed some of the seeds of the common law demise of separate but equal. In *McCabe v. Atchison, Topeka & Santa Fe Railway*, decided in 1914, the Court dealt with an Oklahoma law requiring separate-but-equal railroad facilities. This law, however, said that a railroad could have sleeping, dining, and chair cars for whites even if it did not have those kinds of cars for blacks. The state defended the law by arguing that there was essentially no demand from blacks for those facilities. The Court rejected the state's argument and struck down the law.

The state's argument was, in effect, that it was faithfully implementing the principle of separate but equal. It provided each group, blacks and whites, with the facilities that the group demanded, but not with the facilities for which there was little demand from the group. An analogy today might be an office building in which there are no women's bathrooms on a floor where few women have offices.

The Supreme Court rejected that argument, though, and ruled that the law did not treat African Americans equally: "It is the individual who is entitled to the equal protection of the laws, and if he is denied…a facility or convenience in the course of his journey which under substantially the same circumstances is furnished to another traveler, he may properly complain that his constitutional privilege has been invaded." Notwithstanding the theoretical plausibility of the state's argument, the Supreme Court declined to adopt the more pro-segregation interpretation of separate but equal. Arguably, the Court even cut back on the segregationist logic of separate but equal.

Three years later, in *Buchanan v. Warley*, the Supreme Court did the same kind of thing. The decision in *Buchanan* struck down a law that forbade whites from living in a block where a majority of the homes were occupied by blacks, and vice versa. The Court's reasoning emphasized the seller's right to dispose of his property as he saw fit.

This decision, even more than *McCabe*, is not easy to reconcile with *Plessy*. The checkerboard law in *Buchanan* required a version of separate but equal: instead of blacks and whites having different railroad cars, as in *Plessy*, they would have different neighborhood blocks. If a state could impose separate-but-equal regulation on one form of economic transaction—the purchase of a railroad ticket—why couldn't it impose the same kind of regulation on the sale of real estate? That was the argument the state made in defending its law, and the Supreme Court never answered it. So *Buchanan*, too, can be seen as undermining, however subtly, the logic of *Plessy* and separate but equal.

Twenty years later, after the NAACP (National Association for the Advancement of Colored People) had begun a legal campaign against Jim Crow laws, the seeds that were arguably sown in *McCabe* and *Buchanan* bore fruit. In *Missouri ex rel. Gaines v. Canada*, an African-American student was denied admission to the all-white University of Missouri Law School. Missouri operated an all-black state university, Lincoln University, that did not have a law school. Instead, Missouri law authorized state officials to arrange for blacks to attend law school in neighboring states and to pay their tuition.

The Court ruled that this voucher scheme did not satisfy separate but equal. Missouri had insisted that the out-of-state opportunities for the student were at least as good as those in Missouri. The Court did not decide otherwise; it simply refused to consider the argument that the out-of-state law school would be equal. "The basic consideration," the Court said, "is not as to what sort of opportunities other States provide, or whether they are as good as those in Missouri, but as to what opportunities Missouri itself furnishes to white students and denies to [blacks] solely upon the ground of color." Because a black student, but not a white student, would have to leave the state in order to get a legal education, the Court concluded, there was a denial of equal protection. The Court relied on *McCabe* to dismiss Missouri's argument that few African Americans in Missouri sought a legal education (Lloyd Gaines was, apparently, the only one who ever had up to that time).

There is a direct line from *McCabe*, decided in 1914, to *Gaines*, decided in 1938, and a direct line from *Gaines* to *Brown*. Theoretically, after *Gaines*, a state might still have been able to satisfy the Supreme Court's interpretation of the Constitution by establishing a separate law school for blacks. Given the small number of black applicants, though, that was impractical; in most states, a separate black law school would have been totally infeasible economically. But *McCabe* and *Gaines* were clear in saying that impracticality was irrelevant. What option was left open to states that wanted to practice segregation? Realistically, *Gaines*—while not questioning the principle of separate but equal—left many states with no choice but to admit blacks to the same graduate schools that whites attended.

The other part of *Gaines*—the Court's refusal to consider the argument that out-of-state law schools were as good as Missouri's— might have undermined separate but equal to an even greater degree. By reaching that conclusion, the Supreme Court was, in effect, holding that it was not enough for a state to provide educational opportunities that were equal in every tangible way—for Missouri claimed that it did exactly that. The voucher would get Gaines as good an education as he would obtain in Missouri. But that was not enough, the Court ruled, to satisfy separate but equal. The state had to treat blacks and whites equally in some way that went beyond that. *Gaines* thus suggested that symbolism—not just tangible equality—mattered. That principle was ultimately incompatible with separate but equal.

In the decade after *Gaines*, the Court did not decide any more separate-but-equal cases, but it did invalidate racial discrimination in jury selection, rule that blacks could not be kept from voting in political parties' primaries, and hold that state laws requiring segregation in interstate transportation violated the provision of the Constitution that gives Congress the power to regulate interstate commerce (and, implicitly, sometimes denies that power to the states). In 1948, the important decision in *Shelley v. Kraemer* held that the Constitution forbids the enforcement of racially restrictive covenants in property deeds. Also in 1948, in *Sipuel v. Board of Regents*, the Court held that Oklahoma violated the Equal Protection Clause when it excluded an African American from the University of Oklahoma Law School because she was black. The Court ruled that the case was controlled by *Gaines*.

Then, two years later, the Supreme Court effectively took away whatever breathing room *Gaines* had left for separate but equal. In *Sweatt v. Painter*, the Court held that a law school that Texas had established for African Americans was not equal to the University of Texas Law School. The Court identified tangible inequalities between the two schools, but the Court then went out of its way to say that "those qualities which are incapable of objective measurement but which make for greatness in a law school" were even "more important." The newly established school could not possibly match the University of Texas in those respects.

McLaurin v. Oklahoma State Regents, decided the same day as *Sweatt*, went one step further; it turned entirely on intangible factors. *McLaurin* held that separate but equal was not satisfied when an African American, George McLaurin, was admitted to a previously all-white graduate school but had to sit in a certain seat in the classroom, had to sit alone in the cafeteria, and had a special table in the library. The Court explained that these conditions harmed McLaurin's "ability to study, to engage in discussions and exchange views with other students, and, in general, to learn his profession."

Plessy had upheld separate but equal, and that technically remained the law until *Brown*. But consider what the legal landscape looked like when *Brown* came before the Supreme Court. To begin with, the trend was unequivocal: it had been decades since the Court had actually found a system of segregation that it believed satisfied the principle of separate but equal. In case after case, the Court had concluded that separate facilities were not equal.

Even more impressively, consider what options were available— or rather, were not available—to a state that wanted to take advantage of the separate-but-equal principle and segregate its universities. After *McCabe*, a state could not refuse to establish a school for African Americans on the ground that there was too little demand. After *Gaines*, a state could not satisfy its obligation to provide equality by giving a black student a voucher to attend school in another state—even if that other state's schools were just as good. After *Sweatt*, a state could not satisfy separate but equal by establishing a new all-black graduate school, because any such school, however equal tangibly, could not possibly match the intangible assets of the long-established white school. After *McLaurin*, a state could not segregate African Americans within the established white school. What was left of separate but equal?

Observers at the time were aware that this progression of precedents had left separate but equal hanging by a thread. In *Sweatt*, the lawyers argued that the earlier cases had fatally undermined *Plessy*. After *Sweatt* and *McLaurin*, the *New Republic* said that segregation was "in handcuffs." Some southern law reviews also concluded that those cases meant the end of segregation. The briefs in *Brown*, not surprisingly, emphasized *Sweatt* and *McLaurin*. The opinion in

Brown supported its conclusion that separate was inherently unequal by quoting passages from those two cases that emphasized the importance of intangible factors; the Court in *Brown* said, "Such considerations apply with added force to children in grade and high schools." The *Brown* opinion also cited some psychological research, and that citation attracted a lot of attention; but precedents played a larger role in the opinion than that research.

At the time, *Brown* was not received as merely the inevitable culmination of a common law evolution. The justices themselves apparently did not think of *Brown* that way. *Brown* was vastly more controversial than any of the earlier decisions. There are many possible reasons for this—*Brown* involved grade schools and high schools, not postgraduate education, and the explicit rejection of separate but equal had tremendous symbolic significance. But on the question of the justification of *Brown*—as opposed to the symbolic or political effect it had on the South and the nation—*Brown* rested solidly on the common law approach.

In particular, *Brown* is strikingly parallel to *MacPherson*. A governing doctrine—privity of contract with the exception for inherently dangerous products, or separate but equal—was the established law. For a while, it was applied with a degree of coherence. But then the coherence began to fray. The decisions holding that certain arrangements were unequal (in *McCabe, Buchanan,* and *Gaines*) raised questions about exactly what would constitute equality, just as the New York decisions about scaffolds and coffee urns, while making some sense under the old rule, raised questions about what products weren't inherently dangerous. In both instances, the trend was clear. And in both *Brown* and *MacPherson*, the court could fairly say that it was just making explicit the conclusions that the earlier decisions had arrived at in fact, but had not acknowledged in name: there was no distinct category of inherently dangerous products, and there was no such thing as facilities that were segregated but equal.

Like *MacPherson, Brown* was not dictated by the earlier cases. But the decision in *Brown* could rely on the earlier cases to show, in effect, that the formal abandonment of the old doctrine was no revolution but just the final step in a common law development. The Court of course was influenced by its views about the morality of segregation. That was entirely proper, though, because those views—consistent with the common law process—were buttressed by the lessons of the past. Earlier Courts, trying to apply separate but equal, kept coming to the conclusion that the particular separate facilities before them were not equal. In concluding that separate could never be equal, the Court in *Brown* was taking one further step in a well-established progression. It was acting not as the interpreter of the views of mid-nineteenth-century politicians, but as a court with responsibility for the evolution—in a properly restrained, common law fashion—of the living Constitution.

ROE V. WADE

Roe v. Wade, the 1973 decision in which the Supreme Court held that there is a right to an abortion, rivals *Brown* as the best-known Supreme Court case of the last half-century. But unlike *Brown, Roe* has not been universally accepted. Far from it. In the late 1980s, *Roe* narrowly escaped being overruled by the Supreme Court, and many people still vigorously denounce it. Some commentators who believe that abortion should be made legal nonetheless think that *Roe* was wrong: abortion should have been legalized through the legislative process, not by judicial decree, they say. Even among those who believe that the Supreme Court did have a role to play in protecting abortion rights, there are critics who believe that *Roe* went too far, too fast.

Whatever *Roe*'s merits, that decision has had a baleful effect on debates about constitutional interpretation. Much of the renewed support for originalism since the 1970s, and the concomitant attacks on the idea of a living constitution, have been prompted by opposition to *Roe*, and that is unfortunate. If *Roe* is wrong, that is not because *Roe* is inconsistent with the original understandings: *Brown*, the "one person, one vote" decisions, decisions upholding gender equality, *New York Times v. Sullivan*, and many others are no less inconsistent with the original understandings. Similarly, as *Roe* has survived and been reaffirmed by the Supreme Court (albeit in a modified form) in the face of repeated attacks, critics who believe *Roe* should be overruled have sometimes generalized their arguments into a far-reaching attack on precedent. Such an attack is also untenable; too much of our constitutional system is rooted in precedent.

The debate about *Roe* should, and can, take place within the framework of a living constitution. A belief in the living, common law U.S. Constitution does not commit anyone to supporting *Roe*. But it does clarify the issues in *Roe* and make the debate over that case more illuminating and informative.

When the Supreme Court decided *Roe*, it derived the right to an abortion from the Due Process Clause of the Fourteenth Amendment. That clause says that no state may "deprive any person of life, liberty, or property, without due process of law." There is an obvious problem: the text of the Due Process Clause seems to require just that the government provide certain procedures ("due process of law") before it does things to people. That clause does not seem to confer a substantive right to an abortion or anything else. The initial attacks on *Roe v. Wade* emphasized this point. The Constitution, *Roe*'s critics said, does not confer a right to reproductive choice; the Supreme Court just made that right up and imposed it on the country.

That criticism is too simple. Despite its wording, the Due Process Clause has, for many years, been interpreted to confer certain rights on individuals—in particular, most of the rights contained in the Bill of Rights. That use of the Due Process Clause is a complicated story, but the simplest attacks on *Roe*—the ones that took the form of saying, essentially, that the word "abortion" does not occur in the Constitution—ignored too much about the way constitutional law has developed.

In fact, that simplistic attack on *Roe* has obscured what is most problematic about the decision—both what is questionable as a matter of constitutional law and what is troubling to people who viscerally object to *Roe*. There were two analytically distinct issues in *Roe*, as there often are in a case where a person asserts a constitutional right. One issue is whether the right exists; the other is whether the state has a sufficient justification for overriding the right. The simple attack on *Roe* focused attention on the first issue: whether the Constitution confers a right on women to control whether they will bear a child. But the more difficult issue in *Roe* is the second one: whether the state's interest in protecting fetal life is strong enough to override that right.

A plausible, precedent-based, common law case can be made for a woman's right to reproductive freedom. That right lies at the intersection of two well-established legal traditions. One is that people have the right to bodily integrity. For centuries, the general rule has been that it is illegal—a civil wrong and usually a crime—to touch a person's body without that person's consent. The other tradition is the right to control the composition of one's family—a right that, again, the law has long recognized, with exceptions only for extraordinary circumstances. Both of these traditions reach far back into

American law. They have not been constitutional principles for all that time, but under a common law approach, the long-standing nature of these traditions supports the legitimacy of establishing a constitutional right.

To make the point more concretely, it would hardly be controversial for the Supreme Court to hold that the government may not invade individuals' bodily integrity by conducting medical experiments on people against their will. Similarly, a law that specified that women of child-bearing age must become pregnant, if they are physically able to do so, would strike most of us as raising serious constitutional issues, to say the least. But it is not easy to identify language in the Constitution that prohibits laws like that. What makes them unconstitutional—as they surely would be—are the well-established legal traditions that protect bodily integrity and family autonomy. Those same traditions support the existence of the right recognized in *Roe*. And, both before and after *Roe*, the Supreme Court has, in a variety of contexts apart from abortion, upheld Americans' constitutional rights to bodily integrity and family autonomy.

No right, however, is absolute. The more problematic aspect of *Roe* is the Supreme Court's rejection of the argument that the state's interest in fetal life—or the life of the unborn, as some would say—overrides the woman's right to bodily integrity and family autonomy. I believe that a good argument can be made in support of the Court's holding on this point. The argument would emphasize both the deep-seated, quasi-religious nature of disagreements about the status of fetal life and the fact that abortion laws bear more heavily on women, a group that has historically been subject to discrimination. But it would be disingenuous, in my view, to claim that this argument is obviously correct, or that *Roe* should be treated in a way comparable to *Brown*—as an absolute fixed point of the constitutional order.

Today, the debate about *Roe* concerns not just its initial soundness but its status as a precedent. Here, again, the common law approach to the Constitution does not provide easy answers—which is as it should be; abortion is not a subject that lends itself to easy answers—but it does clarify the issues. *Roe* has been repeatedly attacked, both in and out of court. Several Supreme Court justices have called for it to be overruled. The Supreme Court has narrowed the holding of *Roe* somewhat, but it has repeatedly rebuffed efforts to overrule the decision entirely. Under the common law approach, what is one to make of this history?

The answer, I believe, is that *Roe* should be regarded as more securely a part of the law today than when it was decided, but not as secure as decisions that have become uncontroversial. When a precedent has been repeatedly reexamined and reaffirmed, over many years by a Court whose composition has changed, that should give us greater confidence that the precedent is correct. An old precedent that has never been reexamined, but has simply slipped into the background, has less of a claim on our allegiance than one that has been critically reexamined and reaffirmed; the latter precedent is more likely to reflect the kind of accumulated practical wisdom that the common law approach values.

Similarly, in the late twentieth and early twenty-first centuries, *Roe* has not been eroded in the way that the privity-of-contract requirement was eroded in the decades before *MacPherson* and that separate but equal was eroded before *Brown*. The Supreme Court has allowed abortions to be regulated in various ways: states may impose waiting periods and parental notification requirements, for example. But a core of the right established in *Roe* has persisted.

On the other hand, the fact that *Roe* remains controversial—that many people cannot reconcile themselves to it—suggests that its status is not as firmly rooted as it would otherwise be. This, too, follows from the common law attitude. Protracted opposition, even if it does not prevail, counts for something. *Roe* cannot be put on the same level as decisions—like *Brown;* the one person, one vote cases; or some of the core First Amendment cases—that were initially controversial but have now gained near-universal acceptance.

So the status of *Roe*, under a common law approach to the Constitution, remains solid but not inviolable. In some respects, this answer is unsatisfying. It might be more appealing to have a simple thumbs-up or thumbs-down on a decision like *Roe.* But if a constitutional issue is complex, a theory about the Constitution should not make it simple; it should acknowledge the complexity and explain the source of the complexity. *Roe v. Wade* is not an easy case, and it is a virtue of the common law approach that, while giving us a way to think about the issues raised by *Roe*, it does not treat it as an easy case.

CHAPTER FIVE

The Role of the Written Constitution: Common Ground and Jefferson's Problem

OUR LIVING CONSTITUTION includes precedents and traditions that have developed over time. It is impossible to understand American constitutional law without recognizing as much. But it is also impossible to understand American constitutional law without acknowledging the role that the document itself plays in our system. How can we reconcile these two parts of our constitutional system: a dynamic common law constitution, and an unchanging but centrally important text?

JEFFERSON'S PROBLEM

The place to begin is with Thomas Jefferson's famous remarks about the Constitution. "[T]he earth belongs to the living, and not to the dead," he wrote to James Madison from Paris in 1789. "We seem not to have perceived that, by the law of nature, one generation is to another as one independent nation is to another." So, Jefferson asked, how can any constitution claim the authority to control later generations? What possible justification can there be for allowing the dead hand of the past (the phrase that's inevitably used) to govern us today? Jefferson was not the first to raise these questions, and he was not alone in raising them at the time the Constitution was first going into effect. He was not even the most extreme skeptic. But he was, after all, the author of the Declaration of Independence, and his formulation was the most memorable.

Living constitutionalism is mostly untroubled by Jeffersonian skepticism. The whole idea of a living constitution is that it adapts and changes, so people are not irrevocably bound by decisions made in the distant past. The common law approach of our living Constitution cannot wholly ignore Jefferson's concern, because the common law relies on the authority of past precedents. But the Burkean justifications for relying on precedents—justifications rooted in humility, a distrust of abstractions, and an appreciation for the complexity of constitutional issues—answer Jefferson at least to some extent. Those justifications give a reason for deferring to the past that does not assume that the past has a right to rule us; we defer to the past because it makes sense to do so, for our own purposes. We are more likely to make mistakes if we don't.

Also, importantly, the common law approach does not require undeviating allegiance to the past, as *Brown* demonstrates. To the extent that the Burkean justifications are inadequate, the common law version of the living Constitution allows for innovation. In these ways, living constitutionalism is greatly superior to originalism, which, in addition to its other shortcomings, has no obvious answer for Jefferson.

There is a problem, though. While Jeffersonian skepticism is difficult to rebut, it also seems out of touch with the reality of our political and legal culture. Many people revere the U.S. Constitution. Many Americans consider themselves connected, in some important way, to the earlier generations who wrote and ratified the Constitution we have today—not just the living Constitution, but the document. Allegiance to the Constitution, and a certain kind of respect for the founding and for crucial episodes in our history, seem, to many people, central to what it is to be an American. All of these attitudes are incompatible with Jefferson's kind of skepticism, and as long as those attitudes remain widespread, Jefferson's concern will always seem to be a little like a debating point—clever, hard to answer, but somehow deeply wrong.

More concretely, while we have a living constitution that exists apart from the text and the original understandings—that exists in, for example, the principles that protect freedom of expression and those of *Brown v. Board of Education*—we also have a written Constitution, written by those ancestors whose authority Jefferson denied. And the written Constitution is as important as the living Constitution of precedents and traditions. The written Constitution decides many issues—important issues—all by itself, without the aid of precedents or the common law approach. So while we can put Jefferson off for a while by focusing on the unwritten, living Constitution, ultimately we have to confront his challenge. If we can confront that challenge successfully, we will be able to understand how our living Constitution coexists with an unchanging document.

The answer to Jefferson, in a word, is that our adherence to the written Constitution does not have to depend on veneration of our ancestors or on any acknowledgment of their right to rule us from the grave. The written Constitution is valuable because it provides a common ground among the American people, and in that way makes it possible for us to settle disputes that might otherwise be intractable and destructive. Sometimes, in a familiar formulation, it is more important that things be settled than that they be settled right, and the provisions of the written Constitution settle things. The Constitution tells us the qualifications for various offices, how long a president's term will be, how many senators each state will have, whether there must be jury trials in criminal cases, and many other things. Even if the rules the Constitution prescribes are not the best possible rules, they give us good enough answers to important issues, so that we do not have to keep reopening those issues all the time. This is an immensely valuable function.

This justification ought to satisfy even the most iconoclastic Jeffersonian skeptic. But at the same time, the common ground justification does not *require* anyone to be a skeptic. The real challenge in addressing Jefferson's question is to come up with an answer that acknowledges the reverence that many people feel for the Constitution but that does not make that reverence an admission ticket to full U.S. citizenship. We ought to have an explanation for why we pay attention to the Constitution that does not offend people who venerate the founders and who feel themselves deeply attached to American traditions, but that also includes people who feel no such veneration and no such attachment—people who simply want to live by the rules and do their duty as citizens, while they venerate other ethnic or religious traditions or no traditions at all. The common ground justification accomplishes that—and shows how the living Constitution and the unchanging text are both critical parts of our constitutional system.

THE SANCTITY OF THE TEXT

Even a mild version of Jeffersonian skepticism might suggest that, from time to time, we should decide that particular provisions of the

Constitution are so antiquated, or so indefensible, that we should just ignore them. But one of the absolute fixed points of our legal culture is that we cannot do that. We cannot say that the text of the Constitution doesn't matter. We cannot make an argument for any constitutional principle without purporting to show, at some point, that the principle is consistent with the text of the Constitution. That is an essential element of our constitutional culture. And no provision of the Constitution can be overruled in the way a precedent can, or disregarded in the way original understandings often are.

On many important issues, the text is followed exactly, even when there are serious arguments that the judgments reflected in the text have been superseded. No one seriously suggests that the age limits specified in the Constitution for presidents and members of Congress should be interpreted to refer to other than chronological (earth) years because life expectancies now are longer, or that the provision in Article II, Section 1 that a president "shall hold his office during the term of four years" should now be interpreted to allow a six-year term because a more complicated world requires greater continuity in office. The Constitution says that the Senate "shall be composed of two Senators from each state," and not even the most audacious proponent of the living Constitution would argue that that provision should now be construed to require that states have different numbers of senators because states are no longer the distinctive sovereign entities they once were. The requirement of one person, one vote, has compelled states to abolish their own versions of the Senate; a state legislature cannot, for example, have an upper house composed of two representatives from each county if the counties differ in population. That constitutional innovation was completely accepted, in the face of contrary original understandings and without a constitutional amendment. But to interpret the Constitution to require a comparable change in the Senate is unthinkable. This seems to reintroduce Jefferson's puzzle. Why do we universally accept that the words written by earlier generations are binding?

COMMON GROUND

The answer is that we accept those words, not because we acknowledge the authority of earlier generations but because they serve as common ground in the way I described earlier. Left to their own devices, people disagree about various questions, large and small, related to how the government should be organized and operated. In some cases, such as the president's term of office or the number of senators, the Constitution provides answers. In many other cases, the text limits the set of acceptable answers. This is true, for example, of the features of the criminal justice system: although the Bill of Rights and other provisions of the Constitution do not prescribe exactly what our criminal justice system must look like, certain essential features (juries, witnesses called by the parties, representation by counsel, trials that are not held in secret or at a place remote from the crime) are required by any straightforward reading of the text. Even when the constitutional provisions are open-ended, as in the case of the Religion Clauses, for example, having the text of the clauses as the shared starting point at least narrows the range of disagreement.

The central idea is, again, that sometimes it is more important that matters be settled than that they be settled right. People who disagree about a constitutional question will often find that, although few of them think the answer provided by the text of the Constitution is the best possible answer—maybe none of them thinks that—all of them can live with that answer. Meanwhile, not accepting that imperfect answer has costs. It takes time and energy to reconsider and resettle questions every time they come up. A dispute on a relatively minor issue can spin out of control and create serious social divisions. And there is the risk of a decision that (from the point of view of any given actor) will be even worse than the decision reflected in the text of the Constitution. In these circumstances, sometimes the best course overall may be to follow the admittedly less-than-perfect judgment reflected in the text of the Constitution. Although you and I may have different ideas about the ideal length of the president's term of office, we can agree that a quick and obvious resolution is better than uncertainty or prolonged conflict.

This is what makes the text of the Constitution binding: the practical judgment that following this text, despite its shortcomings, is on balance a good thing to do because it resolves issues that have to be resolved one way or the other. And that is why it is impermissible to ignore the text. If the text were ignored or obviously defied, even in one instance, its ability to serve as common ground would be weakened.

Why don't we just forget about the requirement that the president be a natural-born citizen, as opposed to a naturalized citizen, since that requirement seems indefensible? The answer isn't that we must keep faith with the framers, or anything like that. We don't keep faith with the framers when it comes to seditious libel or sex discrimination or a dozen other things. The answer is that if we ignore that provision, it will be easier for someone to argue that, notwithstanding the text of the Constitution, a particular president who was not reelected should stay in office for a few weeks after January 20 because of the crises facing the nation. And opening up that question could be disastrous. By the same token, every time we plausibly demonstrate that a conclusion we've reached can be reconciled with the language of the Constitution, we make it easier for the Constitution—either the same provision or some other provision—to serve the function of narrowing or eliminating disagreement.

COMMON GROUND AND CONSTITUTIONAL
INTERPRETATION

The common ground approach has implications for how we interpret the text of the Constitution. Other things equal, the text should be interpreted in the way best calculated to provide a point on which people can agree and to avoid the costs of reopening every question. In a sense, there is nothing "inherent" in the text, whatever that might mean, that tells us that the president's "term of four years" means four years on the Gregorian calendar. But interpreting it that way is most likely to settle the issue once and for all without further controversy. The same is true when the text only narrows the range of disagreement instead of specifying an answer. The reason we do not engage in fancy forms of interpretation that would permit us to question the requirement of equal representation in the Senate, or the citizenship qualification for president, or other "textual" resolutions of issues, is that the leading function of the text—to provide a ready-made solution that is widely acceptable—would be subverted by interpretations of the text that struck most people as contrived.

One possibly surprising corollary is that usually this will mean that the words of the Constitution should be given their ordinary, current meaning—even in preference to the meaning the framers understood. The idea is to find common ground on which people can agree today. The current meaning of words will be obvious and a natural point of agreement. The original meaning might be obscure and controversial.

This implication of the common ground approach explains something that might otherwise seem like verbal fetishism. One revealing illustration is the interpretation of the right to counsel in the Sixth Amendment. The Sixth Amendment gives a criminal defendant the right "to have the assistance of counsel for his defence." The original understanding of this provision was that the government may not forbid a defendant from having the assistance of a lawyer that the defendant has retained—that much seems clear from the historical sources. It was no part of the original understanding that the government might have to hire a lawyer for a defendant who could not afford one. But in the celebrated case of *Gideon v. Wainwright*, decided in 1963, the Supreme Court held that, in serious criminal prosecutions, the government must provide counsel for indigent defendants. That rule happens to fit nicely with the language of the Sixth Amendment. But it is just a coincidence—almost a matter of homonymy—that the modern right to counsel established by *Gideon* is supported by the language of the Sixth Amendment. The drafters of the Sixth Amendment might have used some other language to express their intentions, language that would have made it more difficult to find support for the modern right. For example, they might have said that the accused shall have the right "to retain counsel for his defense."

At first glance, it seems odd to use the language of the Sixth Amendment to support *Gideon* when it is only a coincidence that it does so. But if the point is to establish common ground, this use of the language begins to make sense: as long as a court can show that its interpretation of the Constitution can be reconciled with some plausible ordinary meaning of the text—as long as it can plausibly say that it honors the text—the text can continue to serve the common ground function of narrowing disagreement. Original understandings are often hard to ascertain. But once a judge or other official asserts the power to act in ways that are inconsistent with the most straightforward understanding of the text, the ability of the text to serve the common ground function is weakened. That is why it makes sense to adhere to the text even while disregarding the framers' intentions.

Perhaps the most impressive example of this aspect of our constitutional practices is the application of the Bill of Rights to the states through the Fourteenth Amendment, the so-called incorporation doctrine. The Bill of Rights originally applied only to the federal government, but in a series of decisions, mostly in the 1960s, the Supreme Court held that the states must comply with essentially all of the provisions of the Bill of Rights that protect criminal defendants. The effect was to bring about a large-scale reform of the criminal justice systems of the states. These decisions were the culmination of a protracted argument, mostly between Justices Hugo Black and Felix Frankfurter (and their respective followers outside the Court), over the appropriateness of incorporation.

Three things seem clear about the incorporation issue. First, it went from being a subject of intense controversy—one of the most controversial issues in constitutional law between the mid-1940s and the mid-1960s—to being a completely settled issue. The incorporation controversy involved the most divisive matters: criminal justice, federalism, and, implicitly, race. But by the mid-1980s, even the most severe critics of the Warren Court accepted incorporation, and some of them aggressively embraced it.

Second, incorporation came to be a settled issue even though it was not obvious that incorporation was consistent with the original understandings of the Fourteenth Amendment. During the time that incorporation took hold in the legal culture, the received wisdom was that the drafters and ratifiers of the Fourteenth Amendment did not intend to apply the Bill of Rights to the states. Recent historical scholarship has undermined that received wisdom. The important point, though, is that incorporation became uncontroversial independently of the ebbs and flows of historical scholarship. What the incorporation controversy and its denouement reveal about our practices is that—so far as the acceptance of incorporation in the legal culture is concerned—the original understandings were essentially beside the point.

Third, and most striking, despite the fact that there are certain textual difficulties with incorporation, the widespread acceptance of incorporation plainly had something to do with its use of the text of the Constitution. It helped enormously that the Court, in reforming state criminal justice systems, could invoke the text of the Bill of Rights and did not have to rely on principles that lacked an explicit textual foundation.

Since there was no general belief that the framers (of either the Bill of Rights or the Fourteenth Amendment) contemplated that the text would be viewed in this way, and since the text itself doesn't immediately lend itself to that interpretation, why should the textual basis of incorporation matter so much? If we don't care about what the framers thought they were doing, why do we care about the words they wrote? The common ground answer is that, by tying reforms of state criminal justice systems to the text of the Bill of Rights, the incorporation doctrine could operate within the range of agreement in American society. That is, in the face of widespread disagreement about criminal justice, the Court could take advantage of the fact that everyone thinks the words of the Constitution should count for something. People who might have disagreed vigorously about the merits of various reforms of the criminal justice system could all treat the specific rights acknowledged in the Bill of Rights as common ground that would limit the scope of their disagreement. A reform program that had a plausible connection to the text of the Bill of Rights was therefore more likely to be accepted than one that did not.

It is in this sense that incorporation is consistent with the Constitution in a way that a nontextual program of criminal law reform would not be. The point is not that the people in 1789 or 1868 understood that they were requiring the reforms that the Court undertook. As many other examples show, those are neither necessary nor sufficient conditions for a constitutional development. The point is rather that the Court was able to make these decisions and have them accepted not only because the decisions made moral and practical sense, but because they were connected to the text.

The common ground justification for adhering to the text of the Constitution leads to at least one other possibly surprising interpretive practice: by and large, the text matters most for the least important questions. Since the 1980s, the Supreme Court has decided several cases concerning the separation of powers between Congress and the president. Some of these cases have been quite technical, including one about whether members of Congress could compose a board to oversee certain decisions made by a Washington, D.C., airport authority. (The Supreme Court ruled that they could not.) In other cases—concerning whether the president could be sued for money damages, for example, or whether Congress could authorize the appointment of an independent counsel to investigate executive branch officials—the stakes seemed much higher.

The general pattern in these cases, it seems fair to say, was that the more technical the issue, the more the Court emphasized the specific words of the Constitution and the original understandings. In the higher-stakes cases, the Court acted more like a common law court: it relied more on general principles derived from precedents and on its judgments about good policy. At first glance, this seems puzzling. Shouldn't the written Constitution matter more when the stakes are higher? But the pattern is consistent with the common ground function of the text. When the stakes are low, it is more important to settle the matter, one way or another. It is less important to try to get the best answer. The text and the original understandings are natural places to look for a solution.

When the stakes are high, however, the Court is likely to think that it is not enough just to find a way of settling the matter—the function that the text serves so well. When the stakes are high, it is more important to settle the matter right. That is when Jefferson's argument—if we are trying to get it right, why are we allowing ourselves to be ruled from the grave?—is hard to answer. And so that is when the Court will look beyond the text and seek guidance from the living, common law Constitution.

COMMON GROUND, ORIGINALISM, AND THE GENIUS OF THE FRAMERS

The common ground justification for following the text will make sense only if certain things are true of the text. Of course, if the text were entirely open-ended—if it did not prescribe anything in any case—it could not serve as common ground; it would just continue the argument. The more important point, though, is that if the text forced truly unacceptable outcomes on us, the drawbacks of using it as common ground might outweigh the gains. It might still be possible for certain provisions to serve as common ground even if others were disregarded, but we are in a better position to use the text as common ground if we can say that the whole Constitution is binding than we are if we routinely disregard parts of the Constitution and try to insist that only certain clauses are binding.

The common ground justification might seem to be somehow too functional, too cold-blooded. It seems to reduce the Constitution from being a quasi-sacred document, the product of the framers' genius, to being a desiccated focal point, something that people just happen to accept. But it is a mistake to think that the common ground justification diminishes the Constitution.

It takes a certain kind of genius to construct a document that uses language specific enough to resolve some potential controversies entirely and to narrow the range of disagreement on others—but that also uses language general enough not to force on a society outcomes that are so unacceptable that they discredit the document. The genius of the U.S. Constitution is precisely that it is specific where specificity is valuable and general where generality is valuable—and it does not put us in unacceptable situations that we can't plausibly interpret our way out of. There is reason to think that the framers were self-conscious about this. The framers were extremely careful, for example, in the way they wrote about slavery in the Constitution—for one thing, they never used the word. The framers of the Equal Protection Clause of the Fourteenth Amendment did not want to ban school segregation, but they didn't say that in the text of the amendment; there is no added clause saying something like "provided, however, that the separation of the races may be maintained," even though that was apparently what they thought. If they had included such a clause, it would have been much more difficult for the Supreme Court to decide *Brown* when it did, and the civil rights revolution might have been forestalled, with damaging results.

A related misunderstanding affects many widely held views about constitutional amendments. It is commonly said, for example, that the Constitution should not be "cluttered up" with amendments that are too specific or that respond too narrowly to particular current controversies—an amendment to prohibit burning the flag, for example. But we have been willing to add highly specific amendments to the Constitution, such as the Twenty-fifth Amendment, providing for presidential disability, and the Twentieth Amendment, specifying the dates when the president will be inaugurated and Congress will convene. The point is not that specificity in constitutional provisions is bad per se, nor that generality is to be avoided. There is a time for specificity, when we are dealing with matters that it is important to settle, even if they are settled in a way that is not quite correct. And there is also a time for generality that will allow for interpretive flexibility in the future in dealing with highly controversial issues.

This is why originalism is, despite its pretensions, inconsistent with the true genius of the Constitution. At least this is so if originalism is taken to require that the understandings of those who adopted a provision continue to govern until the provision is formally amended. The drafters and ratifiers of the First Amendment may well have thought that blasphemy could be prohibited; the drafters and ratifiers of the Fourteenth Amendment thought that sex discrimination was acceptable. Had the amendments said those things, in terms that could not be escaped by subsequent interpreters, our Constitution would work less well today. But the text does not express those specific judgments. As a result, instead of having to read the First and Fourteenth Amendments out of the Constitution, we are able to read our own content into them—following a common law approach—and then use them to enhance the prestige of the Constitution as a whole. That, in turn, more thoroughly entrenches the specific provisions of the Constitution that serve as common ground.

What originalism does is take general provisions and make them specific. Indeed, that is the point of originalism: to confine judges to specific outcomes rather than leaving them free to interpret the general provisions. Originalists, implicitly or explicitly, claim to be keeping faith with the authors of the Constitution; many originalists make a point of expressing their reverence for the framers. But if they really appreciated the framers, they would realize that a great part of the framers' genius lay exactly in their ability to leave provisions general when they should be left general, so as not to undermine the document's ability to serve as common ground. Making the general provisions specific, as originalists would, undoes the framers' ingenious project.

CHAPTER SIX

Constitutional Amendments and the Living Constitution

ARTICLE V OF THE Constitution specifies ways in which the Constitution may be amended. The very fact that Article V exists is often used as an argument against living constitutionalism. We know how the Constitution is supposed to change, this argument says: in the ways that Article V describes. If we want to change the Constitution, we have to follow Article V. The claim that we have a living constitution is just a claim that we can bypass Article V, and that is illegitimate.

There are several things to be said in response. The Article V process is cumbersome; it requires the agreement of two-thirds of each house of Congress and three-quarters of the states. That is just too difficult a process to be a realistic means of change and adaptation. Some form of living constitutionalism is inevitable, and necessary, to prevent the Constitution from becoming either irrelevant or, worse, a straitjacket that damages the society by being so inflexible. As for the argument that any non–Article V changes are illegitimate, that just begs the question. If you believe—as I've argued—that we do have, and should have, a living constitution, then you believe that there is more to the Constitution, in practice, than just the text alone: the Constitution has more resources, besides Article V, to renew and adapt itself, resources that include the precedents and traditions of the living Constitution.

These arguments are relatively familiar. But there is something more dramatic to be said about Article V—a way in which our experience with Article V, far from calling the living Constitution into question, vindicates the claim that we have a living constitution. Formal amendments, adopted according to Article V, are actually not a very important way of changing the Constitution. The mechanisms of constitutional change that make up the living Constitution—the evolution of precedents and traditions—are much more important. The living Constitution is the primary—I will go so far as to say the all-but-exclusive—way in which the Constitution, in practice, changes. The formal amendments are a sidelight. The living Constitution is the real show. I will demonstrate this by establishing four points.

- First—a relatively familiar point—sometimes matters addressed by the Constitution change even though the text of the Constitution is unchanged.
- Second, and more surprisingly, some constitutional changes occur even though an amendment that would have brought about that very change is explicitly *rejected*.
- Third, when amendments are adopted, they often do no more than ratify changes that have already taken place in the living Constitution without the help of an amendment. The changes in the living Constitution produce the formal amendment, rather than the other way around.

- Fourth, when amendments are adopted even though the society hasn't changed, the amendments are systematically evaded. They end up having little effect until the society catches up with the ambitions of the amendment. In other words, changes come about because the living Constitution changes, not because the written document was amended.

There are two qualifications, but they do not undermine the thesis. I will leave aside the first twelve amendments to the Constitution, which were adopted within sixteen years after the Constitution was ratified. Living constitutionalism is about how constitutional principles change, not about how they get established in the first place. A living constitution is an attribute of a mature society, one in which precedents and traditions have had an opportunity to develop and evolve. In the first years of a new constitutional order, those traditions and precedents may not yet exist. The Bill of Rights and the Eleventh and Twelfth Amendments, like the original Constitution, should be seen as foundational provisions that got our nation under way. The living Constitution took over from there.

The second qualification is that, while constitutional amendments are not an important means of constitutional change, they do serve other functions. For example, several constitutional amendments have served the common ground function of settling matters that are not particularly controversial but that have to be settled clearly, one way or another. The Twenty-fifth Amendment, which spells out what to do if a president is disabled, is an example. This is not a trivial function for amendments to serve, but it is far removed from providing the central means of constitutional change. And, as it happens, a formal amendment process is probably not needed to serve this function. If a formal amendment process were unavailable, it seems likely that our system would develop other ways of settling these issues, such as by ordinary legislation.

Constitutional amendments in our system also serve the distinct function of suppressing outliers. When the nation has reached a nearly unanimous consensus on a subject, the formal amendment process is a way of bringing the stragglers into line. It turns almost-unanimity into unanimity. The Twenty-fourth Amendment, banning the poll tax in federal elections, is an example: by the time it was adopted, only four states had a poll tax. In this way, constitutional amendments do cause changes. But they are changes around the edges, as opposed to the changes at the core of constitutional law that were brought about by, for example, *Brown v. Board of Education* or the evolution of First Amendment doctrine that I traced in chapter 3.

THE LIVING CONSTITUTION AND THE WRITTEN CONSTITUTION

Before now, in discussing the living Constitution, I have focused for the most part on issues that courts address. The reason is that most of the attacks on the idea of a living constitution portray the courts as the problem: to say we have a living constitution is to license the courts to do what they want. I've argued that this position is mistaken, because our living Constitution is a common law constitution that restrains judges better than the alternatives, that is more candid than its leading competitor, and that makes more sense in a variety of other ways as well.

In comparing the living Constitution to the formal amendments, though, it's useful to take a broader view of the living Constitution. There are many provisions of the written Constitution that the courts do not enforce. In general, courts do not decide whether a bill certified by the Speaker of the House as having passed really did get a majority of the votes; courts do not review the House's decision to impeach an officer, or the Senate's decision to remove the officer; and so on. Similarly, there are principles in the living Constitution—important principles—that never find their way into court. They are traditions and understandings—on fundamental issues, of the kind that the written Constitution addresses—that grow up in our society and become solidly entrenched, without ever having been added to the written Constitution and without being enforced by the courts. Or, sometimes, revealingly, they are enforced by the courts only long after they become entrenched in society, and their enforcement is uncontroversial. The courts treat them as constitutional principles even though you will find them only in the living Constitution.

One example—useful because it is uncontroversial today—is the use of property qualifications for voting. Before the Revolution, all of the colonies limited voting to property holders. Many of those property requirements were reduced or eliminated at the time of the Revolution, but many persisted. Then, in several waves of reform in the first decades of the nineteenth century, the states began eliminating property qualifications and adopting what was called "universal" suffrage (although it was limited to white adult males). By 1840, property qualifications were no longer significant, and by 1860, property qualifications had been abolished everywhere. Eventually, the Supreme Court ruled that property qualifications for voting were unconstitutional except in certain limited circumstances. But the Supreme Court did not get around to ruling that way until the 1960s. By that time, property qualifications for general elections had been essentially unthinkable for a century.

Here was a change of constitutional magnitude; it concerned the fundamental question of who could vote. Several formal constitutional amendments address that same question. But there is no formal amendment abolishing property qualifications. That is not because there was some doubt, after 1860, about whether property qualifications were acceptable; they were not. When the issue ultimately reached the Supreme Court, the Court said so. But the principle had been long established by the living Constitution.

This is the kind of episode that is revealing about the relative importance of the living Constitution, on the one hand, and the formal amendment process, on the other, as means of constitutional change and adaptation. There are many others, and they point in the same direction: Article V is, to be generous, decidedly secondary.

CONSTITUTIONAL CHANGE WITHOUT AMENDMENTS

The first indication that the role of formal amendments may be less than meets the eye—and that living constitutionalism is the main dynamic of change—is how often changes of constitutional magnitude occur without any formal amendment.

One example of such a change is the enormous growth in the permissible range of federal legislation. Congress may now regulate subjects that a century ago would have been regarded as the exclusive province of the states: manufacturing, the employment relationship, land use and the environment, agriculture, financial transactions, the sale of consumer products, education, and so on. This expansion in Congress's power is not explicit in the text, and it is not supported by—in fact, it is mostly inconsistent with—the original understandings of the Constitution. It came about principally through an accretion of judicial precedents, which is characteristic of our living Constitution. Indirectly, of course, it came about because of insistent political and social forces that demanded legislation and ultimately would not tolerate judicial invalidation.

The text of the Constitution defines Congress's powers in detail, and the scope of federal power was a principal issue at the Constitutional Convention. But no formal amendment to the Constitution authorized this great expansion of Congress's power. President Franklin Roosevelt, who was responsible for one great wave of this type of legislation, consciously rejected the use of Article V; he believed that he could accomplish his objectives by other means. And, as I will discuss below, the proposed Child Labor Amendment to the Constitution, which would have authorized a particular expansion of federal regulatory power in this direction, was rejected.

The growth in the power of the president, especially in foreign affairs, is another constitutional change that occurred without a formal amendment. Today, the president is conceded broad power to use military force overseas without a declaration of war. The president enters into executive agreements that in many respects have the force of treaties, but without the two-thirds vote of the Senate that is required for a treaty, and sometimes without any congressional participation at all. The courts have consistently suggested that the president can be granted broader powers in the field of foreign relations than in domestic affairs. None of these expansions of presidential authority has a clear basis in the text of the Constitution or the original understandings; all emerged over time, especially in the twentieth century; and all are well established now, without the aid of any textual amendment. They have been established by judicial precedents, but also by the evolution of traditions and practices outside the courts: presidents exercised more and more power, and Congress, and the society generally, did not object.

Similarly, the growth of a federal bureaucracy with the power to make rules and adjudicate cases was not anticipated in any significant way by the text of the Constitution. The Constitution does refer to "executive Departments," but the enormous expansion in the size of the federal bureaucracy, particularly in the twentieth century, is greater than anything contemplated in the original understandings. It, too, was an evolutionary accretion of the kind characteristic of the living Constitution.

Beyond that, the regulatory agency, a central feature of the federal government, only came into being at the federal level in the late nineteenth century; beginning with the Interstate Commerce Commission, created in 1887, Congress established a number of agencies that combined, in some form, executive, legislative, and judicial functions. The New Deal is famous for having greatly increased the number of these agencies, but even by 1933 the administrative state was already well established: the Federal Trade Commission, the Federal Power Commission, the Federal Radio Commission (the predecessor of the Federal Communications Commission), the Commodity Exchange Authority, and other agencies were already in existence. These agencies raised serious issues under the written Constitution. They combined the functions of the different branches, in apparent contravention of the separation of powers; they engaged in adjudication, although their members were not judges appointed pursuant to Article III of the Constitution; and they assessed forms of civil liability without providing for a jury trial, arguably in violation of the Seventh Amendment.

No constitutional amendment authorized either the expansion of the federal bureaucracy or the creation of the administrative state. But the expanded federal government is now a part of our system, beyond any serious constitutional challenge. The constitutionality of administrative agencies has been beyond question at least since the Supreme Court's decision in *Crowell v. Benson* in 1932. In fact, since so many agencies were already well established by then, it seems fair to say that *Crowell v. Benson* essentially ratified a fait accompli.

This pattern of extratextual amendments is not just a twentieth-century development. Chief Justice John Marshall's famous decision in *McCulloch v. Maryland*, in 1819, upheld the Second Bank of the United States and gave a broad construction to the Necessary and Proper Clause of the Constitution, essentially permitting Congress to enact any law so long as there was some remote connection between the law and an objective that Congress was permitted to pursue. Many people viewed *McCulloch* as an example of a Supreme Court decision that amended the Constitution without authorization. James Madison, the most prominent member of the Constitutional Convention, wrote that, in his estimation, the Constitution would not have been ratified if it had included an authorization of congressional power as sweeping as that announced by Chief Justice Marshall in *McCulloch*. But this aspect of *McCulloch* has endured as a foundational constitutional principle; indeed, it has been extended beyond the Necessary and Proper Clause to other grants of power to Congress.

In fact, the evolution of Madison's views about the Bank of the United States shows that Madison—a principal author of the text of the Constitution—was also a proponent of the living Constitution. When Alexander Hamilton first proposed the Bank of the United States, Madison vehemently objected, saying that the Constitution did not authorize such an expansion of federal power. Madison said, at that time, that any alteration in the Constitution would be a usurpation if not accomplished through Article V.

After an extensive debate on its constitutionality, Congress enacted legislation establishing the bank. When the term of the First Bank of the United States expired, Congress rechartered it. Madison, then president, vetoed the bill rechartering the bank—but explicitly on nonconstitutional grounds. By now it was 1815, twenty-five years after Hamilton first proposed the bank, and Madison explained that he considered the issue of constitutionality to be "precluded...by various recognitions under varied circumstances of the validity of such an institution in acts of the legislative, executive, and judicial branches of Government, accompanied by indications, in different modes, of a concurrence in the general will of the nation." In other words, in Madison's view, the bank, which had originally been unconstitutional, became constitutional—because of the living Constitution. A year later, Madison showed that his endorsement of the living Constitution was not empty when he signed the bill creating the Second Bank of the United States.

After Madison left office, the constitutionality of the bank again became an issue; a rechartering was ultimately vetoed by Andrew Jackson on constitutional grounds. In 1831, Madison responded to Jackson's veto by stating even more emphatically his commitment to a living constitution. Declaring the bank to be unconstitutional at that point would be, he said, "a defiance of all the obligations derived from a course of precedents amounting to the requisite evidence of the national judgment and intention." Madison asked:

[W]hich, on the whole, is most to be relied on for the true and safe construction of a constitution; that which has the uniform sanction of successive legislative bodies, through a period of years and under the varied ascendancy of parties; or that which depends upon the opinions of every new Legislature, heated as it may be by the spirit of party, eager in the pursuit of some favourite object, or led astray by the eloquence and address of popular statesmen, themselves, perhaps, under the influence of the same misleading causes[?]

Madison is credited with extraordinary foresight for his contributions to the written Constitution. But the later Madison—who envisioned that "the uniform sanction of successive legislative bodies" could change the Constitution, even without a formal amendment—was equally visionary about the living Constitution.

REJECTED AMENDMENTS THAT BECAME THE LAW

Even more revealing than extratextual amendments that were "adopted" by the living Constitution are the proposed formal amendments that were rejected but that also became, for all practical purposes, part of the Constitution. The Child Labor Amendment, which would have authorized Congress to enact laws about child labor, was approved by Congress and sent to the states in 1924. Congress proposed the amendment after making repeated efforts, thwarted by the Supreme Court, to pass laws limiting child labor. For example, Congress had tried to restrict child labor by invoking its power to regulate commerce among the states; the Court ruled that Congress's power did not reach "purely local" matters, such as manufacturing.

Congress proposed the Child Labor Amendment in reaction to decisions like that. But there was not much support for the amendment. Within a year after it was proposed, it had been explicitly rejected by nineteen states and ratified by only four; by 1932, the amendment was as good as dead, having been ratified by only six states and explicitly rejected by thirty-eight.

But by 1941, the Child Labor Amendment might as well have been added to the Constitution. In *United States v. Darby Lumber Co.*, the Supreme Court upheld the Fair Labor Standards Act, a federal minimum wage law. The Court in *Darby* specifically rejected the reasoning of the earlier decisions that had limited Congress's power under the Commerce Clause. It was as if the Child Labor Amendment not only had been adopted but had been given an especially expansive reading—not just as authorizing laws forbidding child labor, but as repudiating the entire approach to the Commerce Clause that the Supreme Court had previously taken.

More recently, the leading example of this kind of amendment—rejected, yet ultimately triumphant—is the Equal Rights Amendment, which would have forbidden unequal treatment on the ground of sex. A version of the ERA was first proposed in 1923. Congress sent a more recent version to the states in 1972 but not enough states ratified it; it died in 1982. But for at least a quarter-century, the Supreme Court has acted as if the Constitution contains a provision forbidding discrimination on the basis of sex. The Court has required an "exceedingly persuasive" justification for sex-based classifications, and it has invalidated sex-based classifications that rest on what it considers to be "archaic and overbroad generalizations"—such as the view that women are less likely than men to work outside the home. Today it is difficult to identify any respect in which the law is different from what it would have been if the ERA had been adopted.

THE CIVIL WAR AMENDMENTS (AND NON-AMENDMENTS)

Even if the living Constitution can, in effect, adopt a constitutional amendment that was not formally ratified—or even one that was rejected—that does not prove the broader claim that the living Constitution is the primary way in which the Constitution changes in practice. Offhand, for example, it seems impossible to deny the significance of the Civil War amendments: the Thirteenth Amendment, which abolished slavery; the Fourteenth Amendment, which provides for national citizenship and contains the Due Process, Equal Protection, and Privileges or Immunities Clauses; and the Fifteenth Amendment, which forbids discrimination in voting on the basis of race or previous condition of servitude.

In fact, these amendments changed things much less than you might think. The changes in race relations have been the result of other forces—including the living Constitution—much more than the formal amendments. The Civil War, of course, worked enormous changes. And ultimately the nation changed in many of the ways envisioned by the Civil War amendments; today, racial minorities can vote, for example. But it was not the amendments that changed things. The amendments made relatively little difference when they were adopted; the changes they prescribed came about only when society itself changed. The most conspicuous thing about the Civil War amendments is how little they meant in the first century after they were ratified.

The practical effect of the Thirteenth Amendment, for example, was, at most, to abolish slavery only in the four border states (Delaware, Maryland, Kentucky, and Missouri) that had not joined the Confederacy. The Emancipation Proclamation (which applied to states and portions of states "then...in rebellion against the United States")—and, more to the point, the Union army—had already emancipated the slaves elsewhere. As one Union army officer said in 1863: "Slavery is dead; that is the first thing. That is what we all begin with here, who know the state of affairs." In this sense, the Thirteenth Amendment is an example of an amendment that suppressed outliers before they otherwise would have been suppressed. The most that can be said for the Thirteenth Amendment is that it brought about the end of slavery in a few border states a few years before it otherwise would have ended. That is not trivial, but it is a far cry from viewing the formal amendment as the principal means of constitutional change.

The Fourteenth and Fifteenth Amendments present a somewhat different story from the Thirteenth. They did not address slavery, which was no longer an important ongoing institution by the time the Civil War ended. The Fourteenth and Fifteenth Amendments addressed matters of great importance to the post–Civil War South. But they were ahead of their time, and consequently ended up having little lasting effect until their time finally came, in the mid-twentieth century.

The Fifteenth Amendment, barring discrimination in voting against African Americans and former slaves, presents the more dramatic case. The Fifteenth Amendment was not nullified at once. It had important effects in the South until the end of the nineteenth century. In addition, the Fifteenth Amendment helped blacks gain the franchise in the North. But for the most part the Fifteenth Amendment is the inverse of the Equal Rights Amendment: an amendment that was added to the Constitution's text but that did not become part of the Constitution in operation.

The Fifteenth Amendment was ratified in 1870. By the late 1880s, it was being blatantly subverted in much of the South. The subversion usually did not take the form of outright defiance. Rather, southern states adopted a variety of devices, such as literacy tests and poll taxes, that did not explicitly deny blacks the vote but were deliberately designed to disenfranchise them. Where such ostensibly legal means did not work well enough, southern whites used intimidation, subtle or otherwise, and outright violence. By the turn of the twentieth century, African Americans were effectively disenfranchised throughout almost the entire region. The amendment continued to be nullified on a large scale until the middle of the twentieth century.

If you read the Constitution and took the amendments at face value, you'd conclude that the Fifteenth Amendment permanently enfranchised African Americans. It did not. To a limited degree, the Union army, and political changes imposed on the South in the aftermath of its occupation, did; but when those effects faded, the Fifteenth Amendment might as well not have been part of the Constitution. Then, a hundred years later, the Voting Rights Act—itself the product of long-term social and economic forces—enfranchised blacks. The Constitution, in practice, did not change with the formal amendment. It changed only when society's institutions and traditions changed.

The Fourteenth Amendment is a less dramatic case, but in many ways it presents the same pattern as the Fifteenth. The Fourteenth Amendment had one immediate legal effect: it outlawed the Black Codes, laws that had been adopted throughout the South that, by imposing various restrictions and disabilities on African Americans, more or less sought to reinstitute slavery. But massive denials of equality for African Americans, of a kind that the Equal Protection and Privileges or Immunities Clauses of the Fourteenth Amendment were intended to prohibit, persisted until the 1950s and '60s and the civil rights revolution, of which *Brown v. Board of Education*, of course, was an important part.

The noteworthy thing about the Fourteenth Amendment is that, if post–Civil War events had been only slightly different, it might not have been adopted. Congress believed that it had the power to abolish the Black Codes without the Fourteenth Amendment, and the Reconstruction Congress enacted the Civil Rights Act of 1866, which was directed at the Black Codes, before the Fourteenth Amendment was adopted. (President Andrew Johnson vetoed the bill that became the 1866 act, and his veto was overridden.) The Fourteenth Amendment was designed to ensure the constitutionality of the Civil Rights Act of 1866. But had the Supreme Court agreed with Congress about the constitutionality of the act, the

Fourteenth Amendment would not have been necessary even to abolish the Black Codes. Many Republicans at the time believed that "the amendment was simply declaratory of existing constitutional law, properly understood." By "existing constitutional law," some of the members of Congress meant other provisions of the written Constitution, but some took the position that secession and civil war created their "own logic and imperatives"—a version of living constitutionalism.

Although the real change that the Fourteenth Amendment was supposed to achieve did not happen until the mid-twentieth century, still, it might be said, when the civil rights revolution did occur, it was important that the Fourteenth Amendment supplied a textual provision that the Supreme Court in *Brown*, and other advocates for civil rights, could invoke. But even this limited effect cannot be attributed to the Fourteenth Amendment without qualification. When the Supreme Court declared in *Brown* that *state*-sponsored racial segregation was unconstitutional, the Court also ruled, in *Bolling v. Sharpe*, that the Constitution barred the *federal* government from segregating the schools of the District of Columbia. The principle that the federal government may not discriminate is one that neither the text of the Constitution nor the original understandings can support: the Equal Protection Clause applies only to the states, not to the federal government, and the Due Process Clause of the Fifth Amendment, on which *Bolling* relied, was adopted at a time when slavery was legal in half the United States and the slave trade was protected by the Constitution.

The Supreme Court's willingness to decide *Bolling* without a secure (or, many would say, even a plausible) textual basis in the Constitution suggests that events in the 1950s and 1960s would not have taken a dramatically different course if the victors of the Civil War had not added the language of the Fourteenth Amendment to the Constitution. It is difficult to believe that the Supreme Court would have ruled in favor of the school board in *Brown v. Board of Education* if the Fourteenth Amendment had not been adopted—if, for example, there had been a consensus after the Civil War that the Civil Rights Act of 1866 was constitutional even without the amendment, and the Reconstruction Congress had turned its attention elsewhere instead of proposing an amendment. It seems more likely that the Court would have identified some other text in the Constitution as the formal basis for its conclusion that racial apartheid is unconstitutional. (The clause requiring the United States to "guarantee to every state in this Union a republican form of government" would be one candidate.) What all of this suggests is that, despite the appearance of the post–Civil War amendments in the Constitution, the enormous changes in American race relations are the result of other forces, including the evolutionary developments of the living Constitution.

The most conspicuous Civil War non-amendment supports this conjecture. Before the Civil War, the question whether the Constitution permits a state to secede from the union was a subject of lively debate. In the decades leading up to the Civil War, respected political and legal figures advanced serious legal arguments, claiming descent from Jefferson's Kentucky Resolutions, in support of the right to secede. No amendment adopted after the Civil War settled this question, expressly or by any reasonably direct implication.

Yet the question has, without doubt, been settled. The person on the street would say that it was settled by the Civil War, and that person would be right. It *was* settled by the Civil War, even though no formal amendment was added to the Constitution. The Civil War settled the question of the constitutionality of slavery in the same way, and it settled, or, more accurately, began the process of settling, the question of racial equality. The Secession Amendment, by its absence, makes it difficult to argue that the Thirteenth, Fourteenth, or Fifteenth Amendments made as much difference as one might think.

AMENDMENTS THAT RATIFIED CHANGES

There is another category of amendments that seem to have changed things more than they actually did. These are amendments that were formally added to the Constitution only after things had already changed. The change produced the amendment, rather than vice versa. These amendments illustrate, again, how the living Constitution is often the real mechanism of change; changes in the text of the Constitution follow along later.

The Seventeenth Amendment, which provides for the direct election of senators, is an especially vivid example. And the way the Seventeenth Amendment came about alerts us to another important example of the living Constitution in action: how we have changed, without any formal amendment, the way the president is elected.

The original Constitution specified that U.S. senators were to be elected by the states' legislatures. The Seventeenth Amendment, ratified in 1913, formally requires the direct popular election of senators. The direct election of senators may have been a significant change in the nation's constitutional order; it arguably weakened ties between state governments and Congress, and it empowered politicians able to appeal to the public at large, as opposed to insiders who had support only in the legislature. But once again, it would be a mistake to say that the Seventeenth Amendment is responsible for this change. The change occurred, for all practical purposes, before the amendment was adopted. The effect of the amendment was to ratify something that was already accomplished. At most, the amendment just mopped up outliers that were few in number and would probably have fallen into line before long.

The direct election of senators developed in stages, beginning as early as the 1830s. Until that time, candidates for the U.S. Senate typically did not campaign in any significant way until their state legislature was elected. Then they campaigned among members of the legislature. Beginning in the 1830s, however, people who wanted to be elected to the Senate began appealing directly to the voters of the state to vote, in state legislative elections, for candidates who were pledged to support them for the Senate. The famous debates about slavery between Abraham Lincoln and Stephen Douglas in 1858 dramatized this development; those debates, of course, took place before the general public, not before the state legislature, even though Lincoln and Douglas were campaigning for the Senate. Not only did Lincoln and Douglas appeal to the electorate as a whole, but in that election the state parties endorsed their respective candidates for the Senate before the state legislative elections took place. This had the effect of binding each party's state legislative candidates to the party's Senate candidate. In effect, the state legislative election resembled the election of a prime minister in a parliamentary system.

The Lincoln-Douglas election was atypical, but support for direct election increased greatly in the latter half of the nineteenth century. Several constitutional amendments providing for direct election were proposed. Meanwhile, state governments, responding to the sentiment in favor of direct election, also instituted measures designed to bring about direct election in fact even if not in name. Beginning in 1875, Nebraska held a primary election to choose parties' candidates for the Senate. Other states followed suit, and in one-party states (notably in the South), victory in the primary election was tantamount to election to the Senate. In one-party primary states, then, direct election was effectively instituted well before the Seventeenth Amendment was even proposed.

Then in 1904, Oregon took the next step by requiring candidates for the state legislature to include a statement on their nominating petitions either "solemnly pledg[ing]" to vote for the Senate candidate who received the most popular votes or declaring themselves free "wholly [to] disregard" the popular vote. Not surprisingly, nearly all the state legislative candidates took the pledge. In 1909, an Oregon state legislature with a Republican majority elected a Democratic senator who had won the popular election, establishing that direct election existed in all but name.

By 1911, a year before the Seventeenth Amendment was proposed, over half the states had adopted the Oregon system or something like it; in many states, the ballot for state legislative elections stated whether the candidate had pledged to support the winner of the popular election for the U.S. Senate. In at least three states, the state constitution required state legislators to elect the Senate candidate who received the most votes in the primary. Things had reached a point where the following exchange occurred on the floor of the Senate between Senator Albert B. Cummins of Iowa, who favored the Seventeenth Amendment, and Senator Weldon B. Heyburn of Idaho, a rock-ribbed opponent:

> Mr. Cummins: [T]he Senator from Idaho is insisting...that if the voters of the United States be permitted to say who shall be their Senators, then this body will be overrun by a crowd of incompetent and unfit and rash and socialistic and radical men who have no proper views of government. I am simply recalling to his attention the fact that the people of this country, in despair of amending the Constitution, have accomplished this reform for themselves.

MR. HEYBURN: Like a burglar.

MR. CUMMINS: In an irregular way, I agree, but they have accomplished it.

MR. HEYBURN: Like a burglar.

MR. CUMMINS: And they have accomplished it so effectively that, whether the Constitution is amended or not, the people in many or most of the States will choose their own Senators.

The Seventeenth Amendment, therefore, did not bring about the direct election of senators; it ratified a practice of de facto direct election that had been instituted by other means. Once again, the Constitution had found its own mechanism of evolving.

In a way, it should not be surprising that, notwithstanding what the original Constitution says, the direct election of senators was effectively implemented without a formal amendment. The Constitution also envisions that presidents will be elected indirectly, by the electoral college. There is good reason to think that the original understanding was that the electors would exercise independent judgment. But we have long since left behind the idea that the electors decide who will be president. Nominally, presidents still are elected by the electors; but in substance they are elected, on a state-by-state basis, without the electors' intercession. A constitutional amendment specifying that each state's electoral vote total will be cast automatically for the state's popular vote winner, with no room for the electors to exercise their judgment, would have no effect on presidential elections. (Notice that this is different from a nation-wide popular vote, which would be another matter entirely.)

The basic change from indirect to direct election of the president was, like the change to direct election of senators, brought about by state law. In the case of the president, it was ratified by a Supreme Court decision upholding such laws, arguably subverting the original constitutional design. Both of these significant changes were the product of the living Constitution; one happened also to be reflected formally in the written Constitution. But that formal recognition is a detail. The living Constitution was the real agent of change.

AMENDMENTS THAT RESTORED THE LIVING CONSTITUTION

Finally, there have been formal amendments whose main purpose was to restore principles or understandings that had grown up informally—through the living Constitution—and then were overturned, or threatened, by aberrant events.

One example is the Sixteenth Amendment, which authorized Congress to enact an income tax. The Sixteenth Amendment was a direct response to an 1895 Supreme Court decision—*Pollock v. Farmers' Loan and Trust*—which struck down a federal income tax. The Court in *Pollock* had reasoned that an income tax was a "direct" tax, which, under Article I, section 2, of the Constitution, must be apportioned among the states. But *Pollock* was a surprising decision that did not reflect the way the law was understood at the time and did not much change the direction in which the law evolved. Before *Pollock*, the Supreme Court had repeatedly rejected claims that the category of "direct taxes"—a particularly ill-defined notion—included inheritance taxes, taxes on notes issued by state banks, or taxes on insurance premiums. In 1881, just fourteen years before *Pollock*, the Supreme Court upheld an income tax that was imposed during the Civil War but not repealed until 1872.

As a result, when the movement for a federal income tax gathered speed in the late nineteenth century, the constitutionality of the tax was not seen as an important question. The surprising decision in *Pollock* was widely and immediately condemned; one commentator at the time compared the hostility to *Pollock* to the reaction to the Dred Scott case, the infamous pre–Civil War decision that enshrined constitutional protection for slavery. President and Chief Justice-to-be William Howard Taft said about *Pollock:* "Nothing has ever injured the prestige of the Supreme Court more."

After *Pollock* was decided, many members of Congress wanted to go ahead and enact an income tax law anyway—not so much as a gesture of defiance but because they were convinced that the Court would not adhere to *Pollock*. The Court did little to suggest otherwise. A few years after *Pollock*, the Court upheld an inheritance tax, reasoning that it was an excise tax and therefore indirect. In 1908, Taft, in accepting the Republican nomination for president, endorsed an income tax and suggested that a constitutional amendment would be unnecessary both because the Court's decisions might be interpreted to allow some kind of income tax and because there were new justices on the Court.

When Taft became president, he changed his view about the need for an amendment, and in 1909—as part of a package of complex political maneuvers by both supporters and opponents of the income tax—Congress proposed the Sixteenth Amendment to the states. The Senate vote in favor of the amendment was unanimous. At nearly the same time, Congress enacted a tax on corporations that was measured by their income; while the proposed amendment was before the state legislatures, the Court upheld the corporate income tax, again narrowing *Pollock* by reasoning that the tax was not an income tax but an excise tax, in this case a tax on the privilege of doing business in corporate form. After the Sixteenth Amendment was adopted, the Court, in upholding the income tax, characterized the amendment as restoring power that Congress had assumed to exist before *Pollock* was decided.

What happened, in other words, is that society had worked out a definition of the vague term "direct taxes" not through constitutional amendment but by evolutionary means. *Pollock* disturbed the equilibrium that the living Constitution had established. The Sixteenth Amendment—which may not have been necessary at all, because the Supreme Court might easily have reversed itself—restored the status quo.

The Twenty-second Amendment, which limits a president to two terms in office, is a more complicated case, but it can be seen in the same way. The amendment, which was adopted in 1951, was a response to President Franklin Roosevelt's decisions to run, successfully of course, for a third term in 1940 and then a fourth term in 1944. Before then, there was an unbroken tradition—inaugurated by George Washington—that presidents would leave office after two terms. In 1912, President Theodore Roosevelt ran for president in a way that ambiguously challenged that tradition: he had succeeded President William McKinley when McKinley was assassinated, and then had won on his own in 1904. When Theodore Roosevelt ran on a third-party ticket in 1912, he was accused of violating the unwritten tradition; a would-be assassin even shot at him for (ostensibly) that reason.

Franklin Roosevelt's decision to seek reelection in 1940 also may not have been a direct assault on the tradition, because the nation was on the brink of being involved in the Second World War; in 1944, of course, the nation was at war. So the Twenty-second Amendment can be seen as either having restored a tradition that Franklin Roosevelt breached, or as having clarified the tradition. One might say that Roosevelt's decision was comparable to *Pollock*, an aberration that was inconsistent with the broad evolutionary course of constitutional history; the amendment merely restored a preexisting tradition and (it might be said) may even have been unnecessary, because the tradition might have reasserted itself even without an amendment. In either case, most of the work was done by the unwritten norm, the living Constitution. The formal amendment played a supplemental role.

The Constitution of the United States is a tremendous presence in our national life. Many of us venerate it. But the Constitution is more than the document under glass. It has to be, and it should be. No nation can survive for as long as ours has, and can live through so much, without learning, changing, and adapting.

Many people resist the idea of a living constitution because they think the living Constitution means "anything goes"—that talk of a living constitution is an invitation to the people in power to do what they want. But there is no need to see the living Constitution in that way. The living Constitution can, instead, be based on an important set of virtues: intellectual humility, a sense of the complexity of the problems faced by our society, a respect for the accumulated wisdom of the past, and a willingness to rethink when necessary and when consistent with those virtues.

That is our living Constitution. It makes perfect sense to venerate the Constitution and the people who were responsible for it. But it is important to recognize that the Constitution is the work of more than a few inspired statesmen. It is the work of generations of people—lawyers and nonlawyers, public officials and people living private lives—who have grappled with society's problems and done their best to pass what they learned on to us.

Index